Legal Advice Handbook

About the author

Tessa Shepperson is a solicitor in private practice, running her own legal firm 'TJ Shepperson' in Norwich, specialising in residential landlord and tenant law, and employment law. She has her own specialist website for landlords and tenants - **www.landlord-law.co.uk**, and is the author of *Residential Lettings* also published by Law Pack. Tessa is also on the board of directors of a local legal charity, Norwich and District Legal Services, and takes an active part in its management. She lives in Norwich with her husband and son.

LAWPACK

© 2001 Law Pack Publishing Limited

10–16 Cole Street London SE1 4YH
www.lawpack.co.uk

ISBN 1 902646 71 1

Note: In this book, for 'he' read 'he or she.'

Exclusion of Liability and Disclaimer

Table of Contents

Part 3 - Specific Areas of Law (continued)

Acknowledgements

This has been a challenging but very interesting book to write. I have had assistance from many people who have talked to me, provided information, and who kindly checked all or parts of the book for me. My thanks go to all of them; this book would not have been possible without them.

Some people deserve special mention. I am deeply indebted to Delia Venables for her help and, in particular, for her excellent website which has been of great assistance to me in my research. The following have also all been particularly helpful (in no particular order): Steve Wiseman, Manager of the Norwich and District CAB; Steve Dudley, Area Publicity Officer (London, Eastern & Southern Areas) ACAS; Allison McGarrity, CLS Policy Adviser, Policy and Legal Dept, Legal Services Commission; Lynn Evans, Law Centres Federation; Maureen Cleall, Advice Unit Manager and David Beard, both of Norfolk Trading Standards; Olu Ogumowo, Solicitor, Immigration Advisory Service, Norwich; Phil Read, Membership Development Office GMB, Eastern Counties Office; Jean Senior, Solicitor, Saunders and Senior, Norwich; Cheryl Morris, Policy Adviser Family Law, The Law Society; Vanessa Sims, Coordinator, Bar Pro Bono Unit; Juliet Heasman; Katie Lane, Solicitor.

I also wish to thank the staff at Law Pack Publishing, in particular my editor Jamie Ross who has been very supportive throughout. Last but not least, thanks go to my mother and my husband Graeme, who have listened to me talking about this book for the past year and who have helped me in more ways that I can mention.

Tessa Shepperson

To my mother, Patricia Shepperson

Part 1

Introduction

General introduction

This legal advice book is aimed at you, the general 'man or woman in the street', to help you find legal advice either for free, or in the most cost-effective way.

We live in an increasingly bureaucratic and regulated world. We are expected to know and abide by all of these laws and regulations, but they are now so numerous that it is impossible for one person to know and understand them all. However, with every new area of law comes its own body of experts who can advise upon it. With every area of work and practice comes its own regulator and Ombudsman (or equivalent) to regulate it. The answers to your questions are out there; the only problem is how to find the organisation or person who can help you. This is why this book has been written.

The book is divided into three main sections. The first is this, the introductory section. There then follows a section on obtaining legal advice generally. This is divided into two parts: (1) obtaining free legal advice, and (2) paying for legal advice. Here we look at the organisations that provide free or paid-for advice, and what you can expect from them. The longest section is on solicitors and how they operate. A solicitor is probably the first person you will think of when you need legal advice, followed by the thought that you probably cannot afford him! The solicitors' profession is widely misunderstood and this is an attempt to shed some light on how they work, so if it is necessary for you to consult one, you can do so in the most cost-effective way.

The final section of this book looks at most of the areas of law (or equivalent) where the average person is likely to need help and advice. In most cases, there will be some initial comments and sometimes some 'first aid' type advice. This is then followed by a list of organisations that may be able to help you.

Although a considerable amount of research has gone into compiling this book, it is of course impossible to include all organisations that give legal advice or have useful websites. Inevitably some organisations have been excluded; others may not have come to the attention of the writer before publication. Hopefully, the information given in this book will be sufficient, at least, to start you on your search for legal answers. If the organisations given are unable to help you, it is likely that they will in turn be able to refer you to one that can.

Of course, neither the author nor Law Pack Publishing Ltd can be responsible in any way for the advice or information provided by any of the organisations recommended in this book.

This book also includes five articles on different areas of law, which have been chosen because they have been particularly prominent or have had significant changes in the past year. I hope that you enjoy reading them and that they increase your understanding of these current legal issues. Needless to say, any opinions expressed by the writers of the articles do not necessarily reflect those of the author or Law Pack Publishing Ltd.

I hope this book proves useful to you. If you have enjoyed using it, be sure to look out for the next edition in 2002, which will have new articles and totally revised contact information.

The legal internet

An important source of legal information today is the internet, and Internet sites feature heavily in this book. The internet is particularly useful as a source of free information, with many government departments, non-profit organisations, solicitors and barristers, and other organisations having websites loaded with useful information. If you then find that you need to employ a solicitor or other legal professional, these can often be located via the internet, for example, through the excellent Law Society online directory for solicitors, www.solicitors-online.com, discussed in the section on solicitors in Part 2. If the solicitors' firm has a website you can then check them out before contacting them, for example, to see if they deal with the type of problem you have. Many solicitors' sites have articles on various legal topics, and these will also indicate the areas where that firm has expertise.

Also, if you cannot find the right organisation to advise you in this book, most websites have 'links' pages that will help you find other organisations in similar fields.

Be careful, however, about the many sites, particularly commercial sites, which offer to put you in touch with a solicitor. The solicitors will often have been paid to go on their 'panel' and may not have been checked out thoroughly by the organisation, who may have no real knowledge about them other than the application form completed by the firm itself. Also, the solicitor referred to you will not necessarily be close to where you live. There are many other ways of finding a solicitor - the best is by personal recommendation. For further information on finding a solicitor, see the section on solicitors in Part 2.

You will find many internet sites in this book, both in the general sections and in the more detailed specialist sections in Part 3. They have all been visited and selected by the author; however, they may have changed since that time (for better or for worse) or even ceased to exist. The following symbols will give you some information about the nature of the site:

GOV - government site

OFF - 'official' or recognised organisation

SOC - professional society

NFP - an organisation in the 'not for profit' sector

COM - commercial site

ACC - academic site

FOR - foreign site

REC - highly recommended

Note:

GOV   Government sites are those for government departments, local authorities, or organisations that are controlled by either central or local government.

OFF   Official organisations are those that, although not actually government departments, do have an official function. Frequently they were set up by the government but are now independent of it.

SOC   These are societies or associations for professionals and other experts, such as the Law Society.

NFP   Not for profit organisations are generally charitable trusts. Those included will generally offer free assistance, although they do sometimes make a charge for some services and publications.

COM   Although all the sites in this book have free information, those marked COM are provided by commercial organisations, such as firms of solicitors, or individuals offering a service, who are normally providing the free information as a marketing exercise.

ACC   These are sites provided by academic organisations, such as universities.

FOR   When visiting a foreign site, remember that not all of its contents may be relevant to the law in England and Wales.

REC   These sites are those the author considers particularly worth visiting.

If you do not have a computer, you can still access the internet. Many libraries now have internet access, or you can use one of the many internet cafés and bars. You can find the nearest internet café to you in Yellow Pages.

One problem about a book such as this is that some of the references will quickly become out of date, and it will not contain new contacts. You should always ensure that you have the most up to date edition of this book. However, as regards internet sites, the most up to date information can usually be found on the excellent website maintained by computer consultant Delia Venables or on the slightly less consumer orientated but equally good Infolaw Gateway (see later on in this section).

Some internet jargon

URL   This is the 'address' of the website. To use a url, type it in the box at the top of your internet browser.

Link   Internet pages are connected by 'links'. By clicking on a link you can move from one web page to another. This is why it is called the 'world wide web' - it is a web of interconnected links that cross the world. Text links will usually be underlined. Picture links may be surrounded by a black line, although this is now rarely the case. It is more reliable to use the mouse to find links as when your mouse moves over a link a hand icon will appear.

Portal site   A site whose main function is to provide links to other sites.

Note: All contact details and internet urls are correct at the time of going to press. However, it is inevitable that some contact details will become out of date and internet sites will become redundant or unavailable or that the url will change. Neither Law Pack Publishing nor the author can accept any responsibility for this. Neither can they accept any responsibility or liability for the contents of any website referred to in this book.

Obtaining up-to-date information

The following two sites can be used to keep up to date with what is happening on the legal internet. Delia Venables's site in particular is referred to throughout this book as a source of up to date information.

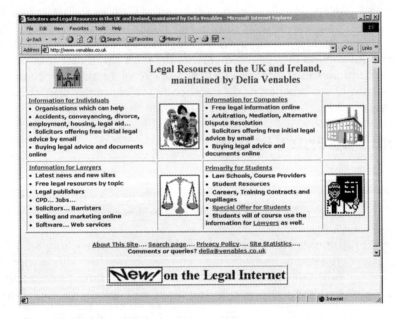

Delia Venables's site

www.venables.co.uk

This site consists of a series of pages of links, sorted by subject. The whole website is divided into four main areas, giving information for individuals, lawyers, companies and students. See the illustration above which is of the main contents page. The general reader should follow the link for individuals. There they will find a link to pages giving sources of free legal information sorted by subject, sites giving information on the UK legal system, sites where free legal information can be obtained online, a full list of all solicitors' firms with websites, and a page with links to firms of solicitors willing to give free initial legal advice by email. There is also a link to legal sites and resources aimed more at professionals but which may be of interest to the general reader. Regular visitors to Delia's site will usually go first to her 'New on the legal internet' page where she lists new legal sites. This page, in particular, is usually updated every few days and is always worth a visit.

All in all Delia Venables's site is a wonderful resource, used regularly by legal professionals (including the author), and should be one of your first ports of call when doing any research on the internet.

Infolaw Gateway

COM
REC

www.infolaw.co.uk
This is a 'portal site' similar to Delia Venables's but aimed more at the legal professional and less at the general visitor. For sites in specific areas of law, follow the 'legal resources' link and then 'A-Z - Legal resources by topic'. An excellent site.

In the following article, Delia Venables discusses the availability of legal advice on the web.

The internet & legal services - now & in the future

The internet is bringing profound changes to the way that information is made available to ordinary people in many fields.

Patients are arriving for their appointments with doctors armed with copious printouts about their ailments and the types of cure on offer.

Members of the public and small businesses are downloading free or nearly-free accounting software from the web and managing without accountants.

People travelling and going on holiday either book their flights and holidays online or at least get information on the sort of costs to be expected - and then cause difficulties for the travel agent who may well not be able to get the same level of bargain through 'normal' channels.

People with a legal problem are researching their problem on the web and are then expecting their lawyer to be able to provide 'just' the extra bit of advice or documentation that they cannot do for themselves.

Indeed, many 'professionals' or specialists providing services that were only recently considered to be available only on a one-to-one basis are finding that they have to adapt or die - and the High Street travel agent, for example, is probably on the way out.

The law is affected by similar pressures, but it does have some special features that mean solicitors are not likely to be an endangered species, just yet.

And from the point of view of an ordinary person, the decision as to whether to solve your legal problem 'on the web' or to use a solicitor is not a simple one - and this book should help you to make an informed choice about this.

Is it legal advice you need, or just 'information'?

There is a very real distinction here. 'Information' is general in kind and is not related to a person's specific circumstances in any way. It might include the description of the stages that the purchase of a house has to go through, the processes involved in a divorce, or the typical levels of payment received for different types of injury. This type of information is very widely available on the web now, and my own site, www.venables.co.uk, describes and lists many of the sources available. Many of these resources are also described in this book - and most of them are free.

Full 'legal advice', however, requires that your own personal circumstances are taken into account. This might cover the detailed working out of the financial provisions of a divorce, the full checking of the vendor's ownership of the house you are buying and whether there is planning permission for a hypermarket next door, or an attempt to determine whether the person you want to sue for compensation is actually liable for the injury. These types of advice are much harder to provide remotely, and without personal contact with a solicitor.

However, the boundaries of what can be done in this way are shifting all the time. Where the 'advice' can be determined by the asking of a fixed set of questions, working through a sort of electronic flow chart, a type of service is becoming available on the web, sometimes free and sometimes available for a fixed charge.

There are, however, limitations to this type of advice. I was allowed to watch a street 'kiosk' offering legal advice on divorce recently in the USA, and the question-and-answer session proceeded very well until the computer asked: 'Is it possible that you are pregnant?' The unfortunate woman undergoing this process broke down and wept at this point, and it was not at all clear how the computer was going to assist her. (I ended up myself, as a totally untrained marriage guidance counsellor, doing what I could to comfort her.)

She did, however, eventually compose herself and moved on in the consultation to where the computer asked: 'How much money do you want from your husband?' which also caused a complete standstill in the consultation. The real answer was 'every penny I can get' but there was not an option for that answer to be given. It turned out that in the USA - as in this country - divorce can be relatively simple if no money is involved - but in most cases, of course, money is involved, and then the topic is by no means as straightforward as it might at first appear.

Another sort of 'advice' that is becoming available on the web is actually not advice in the normal sense, but the provision of documents for your use, based on your personal information. Documents of this type could include the provision of leases for letting out property or tenancy agreements, forms for attempting to recover a debt, forms for initiating divorce proceedings, changing your name, setting up an enduring power of attorney or applying for a grant of probate.

The provision of a will is another example of this type of service, where the computer is programmed to ask you a series of questions about yourself, your family and other people to whom you want to pass on your assets and to then 'draft' the will online.

Quite a few solicitors offer this type of service on their websites and there are also commercial concerns that provide will-writing facilities on the web. Usually, they will include disclaimers along the lines of 'if you have substantial assets where Capital Transfer Tax is likely to be involved, then you should consult a solicitor'. Some disclaimers go further and essentially say that you should not rely on your will without checking it with a solicitor, which does seem to undermine the perceived purpose of the service, which is to prepare your will automatically without human intervention!

Who is providing all this information on the web?

The web is a very democratic medium - the home page of a school student studying law is just as likely to come up in a search as the site of a reputable lawyer. It is very important to consider the provider of the information before relying on it. My own suggestion would be that you should take more notice of information provided on a government site (such as the 'JustAsk' site) or the site of a firm of solicitors, than any commercial concern whose only aim in life, clearly, is to run a 'business'.

Solicitors are controlled by the Law Society, with strict professional conduct rules, and they are much less likely to provide incomplete or incorrect 'advice', whether provided free on their site, or as a charged-for service.

Sometimes, you find that solicitors are providing the advice under the 'umbrella' of a commercial company. They do this in order to be able to offer advice on a limited liability basis (which is not generally possible with advice provided directly by a firm of solicitors) and you then have to decide whether the organisation is more reliable than a commercial company with no solicitors involved!

The future

Where information can be provided simply and reliably on the web, then I believe that, increasingly, this type of information will be available on the web, for free. In many cases, it is available in this way already and it is just a case of finding the most useful resources.

However, I think that one limitation on solving legal problems on the web is that the very nature of the problems for which legal services are required, such as the sale and purchase of property, obtaining a divorce and a financial settlement, settling matters of children and access, writing a will (or contesting someone else's), suing for compensation after an injury, setting up a business or a partnership and so on, are the most important (and dangerous) stages of life itself.

I think it has yet to be proven either that it is possible to provide advice on the web which covers all the potential variations and difficulties in these types of topic, or that it is actually worth saving a few hundred pounds and taking the risk that you have covered the topic properly.

I also think is it interesting that the types of service offered either by solicitors or by commercial concerns, to provide documents or advice directly over the web (without human intervention), have not yet been a notable success. They may be one day - but no-one has made money by providing these services on the web so far.

My own advice to ordinary people with a legal problem is to use the web to research the topic - and to harvest the amazing resources described in this book - but to be careful about entrusting your whole future to advice provided without the assistance of the professional who understands the topic best.

Delia Venables

Delia Venables is an IT consultant for lawyers with a special interest in how lawyers are using the web and how the provision of legal information on the web is developing. She edits the Internet Newsletter for Lawyers, *recently named 'Legal Journal of the Year' by the British and Irish Association of Law Librarians, and also produces a range of training materials, as well as editing her own website at www.venables.co.uk, referred to elsewhere in this book.*

Part 2

General Law

Free advice & information

Citizens Advice Bureaux

NFP www.nacab.org.uk

This is one of the most important free information services in the UK. It is probably the organisation people will think of first when trying to get some free legal advice. It is also referred to in many government forms, and a reference to the CAB is included in most prescribed information on legal notices.

The CAB was set up in the 1930s to empower people to take action for themselves when confronted by problems of bureaucracy or complex legislation. It is a free, confidential and independent organisation, and is intended to be 'of the people and for the people'. By this is meant that it is an organisation which the people cannot use only for their own benefit, but which they take part in to help others, and 'give something back to society'.

The CAB is staffed mainly by volunteers and could not function without them. It is a registered charity and is funded largely by local authorities (now also the Legal Services Commission). However, it also relies heavily on other funding and grants and, as with all charities, funding problems are a constant nightmare. Notwithstanding this, it offers an excellent and professional service and its volunteers are usually trained to a high standard. Indeed, this is often of great benefit to volunteers in their lives, for example, their CAB training has enhanced many volunteers' job prospects.

The CAB is always looking to recruit volunteers and particularly wishes to attract volunteers from a wide range of backgrounds so it can truly be 'of the people'. If you have spare time and enjoy helping people, you may wish to consider becoming a volunteer. Volunteers are needed not only for giving advice but also for reception and other duties. Contact your local CAB for details.

There are many Citizens Advice Bureaux throughout the country and these vary greatly. Some will be large organisations with paid staff (including solicitors sometimes) and will be able to offer a specialised service in many areas. Others, particularly in rural areas, will be much smaller and will only be able to offer a limited service. However, whatever your legal problem, your local CAB will probably be able to help you in some way, even if this is only by referring you to another source of information. Therefore, you should always consider consulting the CAB first about your legal problem(s), as you may not need any other help. However, be warned that CABs do get very busy, so it is wise either to allow plenty of time for your visit or to make an appointment.

A CAB will usually have close links with the local legal profession, many of whom will assist the CAB by acting as volunteers on legal advice rotas and panels, and the CAB is usually well placed to recommend a solicitor if a solicitors' services are required by the client.

You can find your local CAB from the telephone directory or from the Citizens Advice website at **www.nacab.org.uk.**

Adviceguide

NFP www.adviceguide.org.uk

REC This is an excellent website run by the National Association of Citizens Advice Bureaux. It has a huge database of information and you can run searches on almost any advice topic. Highly recommended.

Legal Aid and the Community Legal Service

GOV www.legalservices.gov.uk

Legal Aid started in England and Wales with the Legal Aid Act 1949. Initially, the Law Society administered Legal Aid. However, the Legal Aid Act 1988 established the Legal Aid Board which took over the administration of Legal Aid in 1989. Legal Aid at that stage consisted of several schemes, mainly the 'green form' scheme where financially eligible clients could obtain up to two hours' free legal advice from any solicitor registered to administer the scheme (i.e. most solicitors), and Legal Aid certificates where solicitors could conduct litigation (both civil cases and criminal defences) on behalf of the client. All Legal Aid was means tested. Most types of legal work were covered, with the exception of conveyancing and most drafting of wills, but Legal Aid was not generally available to businesses.

In the 1990s, a new Legal Aid Quality Mark was introduced called (rather confusingly) franchising, and solicitors who obtained this became 'franchised'. They were then able to use the new Legal Aid franchise logo, as well as the old 'picnic table' Legal Aid logo.

Things were changed substantially by the Access to Justice Act 1999. This set up a new body to administer Legal Aid, the Legal Services Commission, which took over from the Legal Aid Board in April 2000. The Legal Services Commission is responsible for the new Community Legal Service and Criminal Defence Service which has also now been set up, and which is discussed separately below.

Developing the idea of 'joined up government', new Community Legal Partnerships were set up consisting of the main funding organisations for free legal advice, i.e. the Legal Services Commission and the local authorities, and the various service providers, for example, the non-profit legal advice organisations and solicitors' firms. Individual partnerships cover Local Authority Areas, so the regional Legal Services Committee of the Legal Services Commission oversees all the partnerships for their designated region. The partnership (or a Regional Legal Services Committee if there is no partnership) will assess the local need for different types of legal advice, and the partnership will then coordinate the funding granted to various organisations (both not for profit and solicitors' firms) to meet that need. The services provided are known as a whole as the Community Legal Service. Thus the many organisations, which once worked in isolation, will now be part of a coordinated group.

The diagram on the next page (kindly provided by the Legal Services Commission) shows how this operates.

The old franchising scheme has now been developed further into a Community Legal Service Quality Mark (or QM). All service providers under the Community Legal Service must have a QM at one of the three levels. These are (1) information services, (2) general help (which may include some casework), and (3) specialist help services. The specialist help standard is the one normally obtained by solicitors and other specialists; the other two are for the other, generally not for profit, advice agencies, such as the CAB (although these can also achieve the specialist

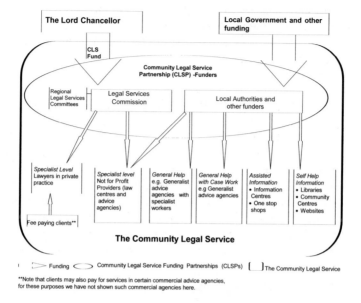

level). All organisations, which obtain any level of quality mark, are able to use the Community Legal Service Logo. The previous Legal Aid and Legal Aid franchise logos are now redundant.

The areas of law, which are now funded by the Legal Services Commission, have changed from the old days of Legal Aid. Claims for money (such as personal injury claims and unpaid debts) are no longer covered, with the exception of medical negligence claims against hospitals and doctors. Clients are now expected to find 'no-win no-fee' agreements from solicitors to finance other money claims. The Community Legal Service is aimed at social welfare problems such as housing, debt, immigration, mental health, community care, and the like. However, probably the largest area of work covered (certainly so far as solicitors are concerned) is family and matrimonial law.

The Legal Services Commission will pay services that are funded as part of the Community Legal Service from the money allocated by the Government to the Community Legal Service fund and/or by Local Authorities and other funders. Services funded by the Legal Services Commission are restricted by financial eligibility rules, but many service providers are also funded from other services to provide work as part of the Community Legal Service, so they can still help you without charging you. Your solicitor or adviser will tell you if you are eligible for help paid for under a Legal Services Commission contract, but even if you do not qualify, many Community Legal Service members will still be able to help you without charge.

Advice is not always completely free. If your solicitor acts for you with public funding and you are successful, you will have to pay the Legal Services Commission back for the money they have paid your solicitor, out of the money or property you recover or keep, unless your legal costs have been paid by the other side. This is called 'the statutory charge'. In most family cases, the statutory charge will not apply to the first £2,500 you gain or keep; it also does not normally apply to the general help scheme. Your solicitor will advise you about the statutory charge, or you can get a leaflet from the Legal Services Commission on the subject (see more about Legal Service Commission leaflets below).

Just Ask website

OFF www.justask.org.uk

REC An important part of the Community Legal Service is the Just Ask website. All organisations which are a part of the Community Legal Service will have an entry, and a link through to their website if they have one. Someone needing advice can search this site to find the most suitable organisation in their area. The entries for each organisation will state the type of organisation it is (i.e. not for profit or solicitor), list the areas of law where advice is given, say whether charges will be made for services and give other information such as access for people with disabilities. All of this information is also available in the Community Legal Service directory which is available at public libraries, CABs and other information points.

Call Centre:

If you do not have access to the internet, you can contact the 'CLS Directory Line' to find your nearest appropriate adviser.
Tel: 0845 608 1122
Minicom: 0845 609 6699

Leaflets

Another new initiative has been the selection of helpful leaflets that have been published by the Legal Services Commission in association with the Consumers Association. These cover a wide range of issues. General leaflets include a general leaflet on the Community Legal Service, a guide to Community Legal Service funding, Customer Services, Representations, the Statutory Charge, and the Special Investigations Unit. Other leaflets cover specific areas of law and are referred to in the appropriate sections in Part 3. At the time of writing, there are 23 different leaflets. They are available in a number of languages and can be obtained free of charge from many advice centres and solicitors' offices, and also:

From the LSC Leafletline on 0845 300 0343
By fax on 01732 860 270
By email on lscleafletline@direct.st-ives.co.uk
Online at www.legalservices.gov.uk & www.justask.org.uk.

Other new initiatives

The Legal Services Commission is also developing other methods of delivery of legal services and there are currently a number of pilot projects. For example, one of these is the development of a Housing Possession Court Duty Scheme to give advice at court for people who are having their homes repossessed by their landlords or mortgage lender. They are also running a small pilot scheme for telephone advice and are researching the possibility of providing more information online. No doubt over time some of these pilots will become mainstream and other initiatives will be developed to improve the provision of legal advice within the service.

The Community Legal Service is a new concept that has only recently been introduced and will probably take many years to develop fully. Despite initial scepticism from the profession, and the inevitable teething problems, it appears to be working reasonably well within its parameters. However, many of its services (particularly the specialist services funded by the Legal Services Commission) are only generally available to people on benefit or a low income, and this inevitably leaves a large sector of the population who will have to pay the full price for legal services, which they are often unable to afford. If you fall into this category, hopefully this book will be of some assistance to you.

The Criminal Defence Service ⟨⟩

From 2 April 2001, the Criminal Defence Service replaced the old system of Criminal Legal Aid. This is, as before, largely provided by firms of solicitors who specialise in criminal advocacy work. However, only firms that have a contract with the Legal Services Commission can be part of the service. The Legal Service Commission is also piloting a Public Defender Service staffed by salaried defenders in various parts of the country. Organisations, which are part of the Criminal Defence Service, will be entitled to use the CDS logo (see above).

Further information about the Criminal Defence Service can be found in the 'Crime' section in Part 3.

Law Centres

NFP www.lawcentres.org.uk

Law Centres were conceived in the 1960s and the first Law Centre, North Kensington, was set up in 1970. There are currently in the region of 50 Law Centres in England, Wales and Northern Ireland. They aim to work within their local community, not only to provide for the legal needs of the poor and disadvantaged, but also to try to combat social exclusion, tackle the worst aspects of poverty and to promote active citizenship. They traditionally cover the 'social welfare' areas of work such as housing, welfare rights, employment, education law, disability rights, immigration and nationality, community care and human rights. Some Law Centres also deal with juvenile crime and domestic violence. However, they do not do any of the commercial or other work, such as conveyancing, adult crime or personal injury work, generally covered by private solicitors. All Law Centres are non-profit making and independent.

The idea behind Law Centres was to fill the gaps in provision, to bring the law to the people and to have a different approach. Law Centres tend to operate in a much more informal and approachable way than traditional legal offices. As well as dealing with general case work, they will bring test cases and group actions to develop the law, as well as applying for judicial review and taking cases to the European Courts. The ability of Law Centres to use their legal skills creatively in this way is one of their main characteristics and is what makes them an essential part of the legal landscape.

Law Centres work within their local community and will often offer legal advice for community projects. They will provide speakers for local organisations such as women's groups, youth workers and tenants' associations, and will also offer training to local organisations, as well as producing leaflets on legal topics. These will often be produced in the language of the local community, if this is not English. They will also offer help and support to other advice agencies and are an important part of the Community Legal Service.

Law Centres are always staffed by several solicitors and/or barristers, as well as support staff and paralegals. They will always try to employ local people if possible, particularly those who speak the local language if there are many local non-English speakers. They exist mostly in areas where there is a concentration of disadvantaged people.

As with all not for profit organisations, funding is a perennial problem. A large part of their funding now comes from the Legal Services Commission, as well as the Community Fund and local authorities.

All Law Centres are members of the Federation of Law Centres, which works to coordinate their efforts and to set up new Law Centres wherever possible.

A full list of all Law Centres with contact details can be found at the end of this book.

Solicitors' free advice sessions

Many solicitors now offer free advice sessions, or surgeries. These are useful for preliminary advice or simple matters where a half-hour consultation will be sufficient. Of course, the solicitors are hoping to take you on after the free session as a paying client. If this is what you want, the free advice session can give you an opportunity to decide whether you want that particular solicitor to act for you. You can find out which solicitors offer free advice sessions from their yellow pages ads and many of them will also advertise their service in the local paper.

Solicitors' free email advice

Many solicitors with websites are willing to provide free initial advice by email. Again, they are really hoping that you will become a 'proper' client. However, they will generally provide some useful help and advice. Delia Venables provides a list of firms that are prepared to do this on her website at **www.venables.co.uk**. If you take advantage of this service, be sure to give the solicitors all the details relevant to your case, as they will generally only be prepared to give one free advice email. Any further advice will probably have to be paid for.

The Bar Pro Bono Unit

NFP www.barprobono.org.uk

For the past five years, barristers have operated a Pro Bono Unit where the general public can obtain the services of a barrister for free. An application must be made to the unit in London where their management committee will review it. If the application is accepted, the Unit will then find a barrister for the client.

In order to get help, applicants must meet the following criteria:

- The case must have legal merit and deserve pro bono assistance.
- Applicants must normally be financially ineligible for Legal Aid and must demonstrate that they are unable to pay for the assistance they require and have no other form of help with legal expenses (e.g. from insurance or a trade union).
- The case must require the skills of an experienced barrister.
- Preparation, advice and representation should normally be capable of completion within three working days, although in exceptional cases assistance can be given beyond that time limit.
- There should be no other source of help.

Where the applicant is a litigant-in-person, an assessment will be made as to whether a solicitor is also required to assist with the case.

Wherever possible the applicant should make an application with the assistance of a solicitor or other advice agency who is willing to remain involved in the case. In exceptional cases, the Unit may be able to find a solicitor to act on a pro bono basis.

The unit has a website with useful information about the service, and you can also print off the application form.

7 Grays Inn Square
Grays Inn
London WC1R 5AZ
Tel: 020 7831 9711
Fax: 020 7831 9733
Email: enquiries@barprobonounit.f9.co.uk

Government & local authorities

Very often legal advice or information can be obtained from the relevant government or local government departments. For example, if you are a tenant with a problem with your landlord, you can speak to the tenancy relations officer at your local authority.

If your problem relates to government regulations or misadministration, officials will usually be able to give information, if only on their complaints scheme. It may also be worth contacting your local Councillor or MP who can often give helpful advice and point you in the right direction. Sometimes, they are able to 'pull strings' to assist you, for example, if officials are being unnecessarily obstructive. MPs hold regular surgeries in their constituencies and these are generally advertised in the local press. You can find out the name and contact details for your local Councillor by telephoning your local authority, or you may find them on your local authority website.

All government departments and local authorities now have websites and these are often very large containing vast amounts of information. They can all be located via the UK Online service discussed below. The main government department sites, such as the Department of Trade and Industry and the Home Office sites in particular, are extremely useful and contain extensive information on legislation, plus useful links to outside sources.

If you are unhappy about the service provided by a government department or service, there is normally an ombudsman you can complain to who will be able to investigate your complaint free of charge.

UK Online

GOV www.ukonline.gov.uk

This is the main starting point for all government and local authority websites. The site starts by asking if you want information on England, Scotland, Wales or Ireland and whether you want information in English or Welsh. You are then given choices to follow helping you to find the information you want. For example, if you choose 'quick find' and then 'Central Government Services', you will be taken to an alphabetical index of all government services. If you choose 'life episodes', you will find information and relevant links for various types of common life situation, such as having a baby or dealing with crime. If you follow the 'Citizenspace' link, you can find out about government consultations and email the relevant department with your views, and also participate in online discussions. This is a huge site and system and it will probably take you some time to find your way around.

The Parliamentary Ombudsman and the Health Service Ombudsman

OFF   www.ombudsman.org.uk

These are two separate Ombudsmen but they are covered together on the same website and address. They investigate independent complaints about government departments and the health service.

The Parliamentary Ombudsman investigates complaints that injustice has been caused by misadministration on the part of the government departments or other public bodies. The Health Service Ombudsman investigates complaints that a hardship or injustice has been caused by the NHS's failure to provide a service, by a failure in service, or by misadministration. Both services are free, but neither Ombudsman has to investigate all cases referred to him. There are some types of complaint he will not be able to deal with. For further information, see the website.

Millbank Tower
Millbank
London SW1P 4QP

Parliamentary Ombudsman
Tel: 0845 015 4033, 020 7217 4163
Fax: 020 7217 4160
Email: OPCA.Enquiries@ombudsman.gsi.gov.uk

Health Service Ombudsman
Tel: 020 7217 4051
Fax: 020 7217 4000
Email: OHSC.Enquiries@ombudsman.gsi.gov.uk

Change of address

GOV   www.changeofaddress.gov.uk

This is a government service that you can use to inform all government departments of your change of address.

The Local Government Ombudsman

GOV www.lgo.org.uk

This is the organisation you can contact if you experience injustice as a result of misadministration at local government level in England. The website has a guide on how to complain to the Ombudsman and there is a form online you can use. There are three Local Government Ombudsmen in England and they each deal with complaints from different parts of the country. They investigate complaints about most council matters including housing, planning, education, social services, consumer protection, drainage and council tax. The Ombudsmen can investigate complaints about how the council has done something, but they cannot question what a council has done simply because someone does not agree with it. If you have a complaint, you should complain first to the local government directly, either yourself or via your local councillor. If it is not resolved properly within a reasonable time, then go to the Ombudsman. If you need help with making your complaint, there is an advice line you can ring.

Adviceline: 0845 602 1983, open between 9am and 4.30pm Monday to Friday.

The three English Local Government Ombudsmen and the areas they cover are as follows:

London boroughs north of the river Thames (and including Richmond), Essex, Kent, Surrey, Suffolk, East and West Sussex:

Mr E B C Osmotherly CB
21 Queen Anne's Gate
London SW1H 9BU
Tel: 020 7915 3210
Fax: 020 7233 0396

The West Midlands (except Coventry City), Staffordshire, Shropshire, Cheshire, Derbyshire, Nottinghamshire, Lincolnshire and the north of England (except the Cities of York and Lancaster):

Mrs P A Thomas
Beverley House

17 Shipton Road
York YO30 5FZ
Tel: 01904 663 200
Fax: 01904 663 269

*London boroughs south of the river Thames (except Richmond),
the Cities of York, Lancaster and Coventry, and the rest of England
(not included in the areas of Mr Osmotherly and Mrs Thomas):*

Mr J R White
The Oaks No 2
Westwood Way
Westwood Business Park
Coventry CV4 8JB
Tel: 024 7669 5999
Fax: 024 7669 5902

Local Ombudsman - Wales

GOV   www.ombudsman-wales.org
The Welsh equivalent of the Local Government Ombudsman. This
is an independent Commissioner appointed by the Crown, whose
role is to investigate complaints against certain local authorities in
Wales.

Mr Elwyn Moseley
Derwen House
Court Road
Bridgend CF31 1BN
Tel: 01656 661 325
Fax: 01656 658 317
Email: enquiries@ombudsman-wales.org

Regulatory bodies

Many of the organisations originally set up to regulate and enforce
legislation have developed an advisory function and will provide help and
information if asked.

Trading Standards - see 'Consumer problems' section.

Office of Fair Trading - see 'Consumer problems' section.

Health & Safety Executive - see 'Employment law' section.

Trade Unions

Trade Unions were initially formed in the nineteenth century to be a self-help and support group for employees, and to fight against the appalling working conditions endemic at that time.

They probably reached the zenith of their power in the 1970s, since which time they have became less dominant in the political field. However, they are still, particularly the larger unions, extremely powerful organisations.

Strictly speaking Trade Unions are not 'free', as you have to pay a subscription to be a member. However, once you are a member, you are able to take advantage of the many services offered by Unions to their members.

The particular services on offer will depend upon which Union you belong to, as they are all different. There are over 70 unions in existence, ranging from the very large to the small. The following services, however, are generally on offer:

- Legal advice and assistance on employment matters. All unions should offer this. For further information, see the Employment section below.

- Assistance with Personal Injury claims. This may be just for accidents at work. However, many Unions will also offer free advice on road accident claims and possibly other types of claim as well. Sometimes, cover will also be given to the member's family. Frequently, assistance will also be given for criminal injury claims.

- A general free legal advice scheme. This will often be telephone advice on all legal matters.

- Free wills.

- Training on employment related matters such as health and safety at work. This is usually available mainly to those who wish to become Union representatives

- Other services. These can include free or low cost insurance, other financial services such as pensions, mortgages and investment advice, holiday services and, sometimes, convalescent facilities.

- Generally, if you have a problem, your local Union representative or local office will try to help you. If they are unable to assist you themselves, they may be able to put you in touch with someone else who can.

If you are an employee, in whatever industry and at whatever level (from lowly clerk to chief executive), it is worth considering joining a Union. Even if you are the only Union member in your firm, you will still gain from your membership, as you will have access to a source of information and support about employment matters and can seek help if you have any employment problem.

If there is a recognised Union at your firm, then this is the best Union to join. However, if your firm does not have Union recognition, you may find it difficult to decide which of the many Unions is the right one for you. Many Unions are specific for particular types of employment, for example, the actors' Union Equity.

Perhaps the best way forward, if you do not know which Union to join, is to contact the TUC. They can advise you on which unions cater for your type of job and make a recommendation. Alternatively, contact all the Unions that you think may be suitable, ask them to send you a joining pack, and then consider which offers the best value.

TUC Online

OFF www.tuc.org.uk

The Trade Union Congress is the umbrella group to which most unions are affiliated. For guidance on which Union to join, follow the link to 'Britain's Unions'. There is an online form you can fill in and email to get advice on the most suitable Union for you, or there is a link to a list of all the affiliated Unions. If you do not have internet access, ring the 'know your rights' telephone line. The site also has extensive information about the work of the TUC, a 'know your rights' section with much information about rights in the workplace and a section for students.

Congress House
Great Russell Street
London WC1B 3LS
Tel: 020 7636 4030
Know your rights telephone line: 0870 600 4882
(National rate, 8am - 10pm)

Other Unions: Because there are so many of them, it is not possible to provide information about any specific Union. However, you will find links to all the Union sites from the TUC Online site.

Insurance and other telephone helplines

You may find that you have already got access to free telephone advice from your insurer, or from your membership of some other organisation such as your Trade Union. It is always worth contacting these, as the advice can often be helpful.

The internet

Here are some other useful general internet sites providing a wide range of legal information and services.

NB: See also Delia Venables and Nick Holmes' 'Infolaw' sites described in Part 1.

The Directory of Ombudsmen

SOC www.bioa.org.uk

This is a useful website on Ombudsmen who are members of the British and Irish Ombudsman Association. It has helpful information about Ombudsmen and a list of Ombudsmen you can use, with a summary of their services and contact details. You can find Ombudsmen in both the UK and Ireland. Many of the Ombudsmen listed are also mentioned in this book, but not all, so this site is well worth a visit.

The Court Service

GOV www.courtservice.gov.uk

REC If you are contemplating bringing legal proceedings or if someone has started an action against you, you will find helpful information leaflets at your local County Court office. These leaflets are also to be found on the Court Service website, which also has all the forms you are likely to need, plus the Civil Procedure Rules, a database of cases and much more information. If you are unfamiliar with legal procedure, there is a very helpful information section that includes a glossary of legal terms.

Everyform

COM www.everyform.net

This useful site has hundreds of forms, mostly legal, which you can download for free.

Interactive Law

COM www.interactive-law.co.uk

This organisation has a number of linked websites covering different legal topics. For example, there are sites on consumer law, Scottish law and employment law. Most of these sites have useful information on the site topic. You can also email a local solicitor for advice.

Compact Law

COM www.compactlaw.co.uk

This is a useful site with a series of questions and answers on some of the most important areas of law for the ordinary person, such as consumer problems, relationships, housing and employment. You can also purchase documents online, use the site to help find a solicitor and sign up to get free legal updates by email. The organisation and website were formerly known as Law Rights.

Duhaime's Law Dictionary

COM
FOR www.duhaime.org/diction.htm

This is an online law dictionary; very useful if you come across a legal term you do not understand. Although provided by a Canadian firm, most of the legal terms are the same as ours.

Law on the Web

COM www.lawontheweb.co.uk

A very useful website with information on various legal topics, contact details, legal news and a 'legal fun' page to cheer you up. Well worth a visit.

Law Pack Publishing

COM www.lawpack.co.uk

Law Pack Publishing produce a varied range of do-it-yourself legal publications which will enable you to handle your own straightforward legal transactions, at a fraction of the cost of a solicitor. The site also provides you with the number of a legal helpline which you can call to speak to a qualified solicitor in confidence.

Paying for legal advice & services

Solicitors

Although there is a lot you can do to help yourself, sometimes there is no alternative but to use a solicitor. If so, it is best to recognise this early on, because if you continue to struggle by yourself, you may find that you have only made things worse and that it will cost you more to put things right than if you had used a solicitor from the start. If you need to instruct a solicitor, this section will help you do so in the most cost-effective way. However, first we will discuss solicitors, solicitors' firms and how they operate, and some of the terms used that may confuse you.

Some jargon explained

Here are some of the general terms commonly used by solicitors which may puzzle you:

Retainer: This term is used to describe the situation where a solicitor is acting for a client, e.g. 'we have a retainer from Mr X'. It covers the whole relationship between the solicitor and his client. However, sometimes it is also used as shorthand for 'retainer fee', i.e. money paid by a client to solicitor to secure his services.

Instructions: When solicitors are acting for a client they will say that they have 'instructions' from that client. This reflects the fact that a solicitor can only carry out work if he is authorised to do it by the client - if the client has 'instructed' him to do it.

Pro bono: This is short for 'pro bono publico' and means unpaid or charitable work. Solicitors do more pro bono work than most people realise.

Litigation: Taking legal action through the courts.

Disbursements: Expenses that have to be paid in connection with a case or piece of work. For example, court fees or fees paid to the Land Registry.

Contentious and non-contentious: Contentious work is essentially litigation and non-contentious work is all the other work that does not involve court action.

Private client work: This generally means work for individuals, rather than for limited companies or PLCs.

Client care letter: The solicitors' practice rules provide that solicitors should give clear information to clients about costs and other matters, and operate a complaints procedure. This information is usually given to clients in a standard letter called a client care letter. A client care letter should be provided to all new clients.

You may sometimes find that your solicitor uses words that you do not understand, or that he does not explain things clearly. Some solicitors are so steeped in the law and its concepts that they find it difficult to appreciate that other people are not. You should not be afraid to ask him to explain things to you, several times if necessary. After all, he is supposed to be advising you, so it is not unreasonable to insist that you understand his advice. Do not agree to anything until you are certain that you have understood.

The solicitor explained

A person is 'admitted' as a solicitor after having completed his training. This usually involves obtaining a law degree or equivalent, passing the professional examinations and then spending a period of time (usually two years) as a trainee solicitor. There are other routes for qualification - most commonly by legal executives taking further training. Once admitted, a solicitor will then be added to the 'roll' of solicitors kept by the Master of the Rolls (the most senior Judge in the Court of Appeal). To practice as a solicitor, a solicitor will normally need to have a 'practising certificate' which is obtained from the Law Society annually on payment of the relevant fee and on satisfying the Law Society's various requirements for practice (e.g. that he has complied with the continuing education requirements and is covered by professional indemnity insurance). Most solicitors will work in solicitors' firms (or solicitors' practices as they are also called), but some will work as 'employed' solicitors in local government, the civil service or industry. All big companies will normally have a legal department, for example, the utilities and the BBC. Solicitors are also often employed by charities and, of course, Law Centres.

Although in this book 'he' is used throughout to represent both sexes, it should be noted that currently over half the intake of new solicitors are women.

From partners to paralegals

Solicitors usually operate as partnerships. Sometimes the partners are the founders of the firm, sometimes solicitors are made partners - usually after working at the firm for a number of years. There are two sorts of partners, equity partners who are the real owners of the firm and who take a share of the profits (if any), and salaried partners who are partners in name only and who get paid a salary. Usually a list of the partners' names can be found on solicitors' firms' headed paper. Solicitors who practise on their own without partners are called sole practitioners.

A firm will usually employ other solicitors who are known as 'assistant' solicitors. Some of these are called 'associates'. This means that they have more status within the firm and are likely to be made a partner within a few years.

Firms will also often employ non-solicitors to do legal work. These are as follows:

- **Legal executives:** Someone who is a member of the Institute of Legal Executives and who has passed their exams (sometimes a legal executive will then do further training and qualify as a solicitor).

- **Licensed conveyancers:** Someone who has passed the exams set by the Council for Licensed Conveyancers and who is licensed by them to carry out conveyancing work. They can set up their own firms but many work in solicitors' practices.

- **Paralegals (who used to be called 'solicitors' clerks'):** People who do legal work but who do not have any formal legal qualifications. Notwithstanding this, many of them are extremely knowledgeable and sometimes better than many solicitors in their particular area of work.

- **Trainee solicitors (who used to be called 'articled clerks'):** People who are doing the final 'practical experience' stage of their solicitor's training.

Staff who earn money for the firm are generally referred to as 'fee-earners', as opposed to other support staff such as receptionists and secretarial staff. Fee-earners will include trainee solicitors, if these are employed at a firm.

Teams - or 'every time I ring up about my case I speak to someone different'

Many firms, particularly the larger firms, will operate as 'teams'. A team will generally consist of a partner, one or more assistant solicitors, one or more legal executives and paralegals, secretaries and perhaps a trainee solicitor. They will all work on cases together. For example, the partner may take initial instructions from a client, legal research may be done by the trainee, documentation drafted by an assistant solicitor, and everything checked by the partner before it is sent out.

This is a very good way of working. The partner's greater experience can be used for the benefit of more cases, and all members of the team will be able to discuss the case with each other and help one another. This generally results in a better service for the client. However, clients often become upset if they find that more than one person is working on their case and feel that their work is being passed from pillar to post around the office. Although it cannot be denied that this does sometime happen, particularly with an unpopular client, if your case is genuinely being dealt with on a team basis, you should have nothing to worry about.

Types of solicitors' firms

There are many different types of firm of solicitor, and when choosing a solicitor you need to consider which is the most appropriate for you. Most firms will fall into one of the following categories:

- **Large firms:** The very biggest firms are extremely large indeed and have hundreds of partners. These firms will have several offices, not only in England and Wales, but often also in Europe and around the world. Most of their work will be for industry, government and local authorities, and other large organisations. However, they may also offer services that are suitable for smaller firms or individuals. Generally their lawyers will be specialists in their field of work, their staff will be trained to a high standard, and they will have wonderful facilities, for example, IT and library facilities. Their service will normally be excellent but extremely expensive. Think carefully before instructing a solicitor in one of these firms. However, if you need very good advice in one of the more esoteric areas of law, such as intellectual property, tax or planning law, they may be your best choice.

- **City firms:** This normally means 'City of London' and implies that the firm acts mainly for corporate clients. Most of the large firms will have a city office. Some city firms will do private client work but they will generally be expensive.

- **High Street firms:** These firms are usually of medium size, about five to twenty partners, and will generally cater for their local community - local businesses and individuals. Some of them may do legal aid work. This type of firm is often the best choice for the small business or individual, particularly if the type of work that needs to be done is 'run of the mill' - conveyancing, wills, personal injury claims, matrimonial or family problems, etc.

- **Small firms:** These are sole practitioners or firms with two to five partners. Most firms in rural areas or small towns are small, as there will not be sufficient work to support a large firm. These firms, particularly in rural areas, will usually be fairly generalist and concentrate on conveyancing and wills. Small firms in larger towns and cities may specialise in particular areas of work. Be wary of solicitors in small firms who take on all types of work. If the solicitor has a wide experience he may well be very good; however, he may be taking on more than he can manage.

- **Sole practitioners:** These are solicitors who practice without partners. They vary from one solicitor working from home, to firms with quite a large staff who only differ from the average high street firm by the fact that the firm is owned by one solicitor rather than a partnership. Sole practitioners constitute about 42 per cent of all solicitors' firms but only about seven per cent of solicitors. Most sole practitioners set up in practice because they want to be independent and to have the freedom to develop their work in a way that they could not do within the confines of a larger firm. However, a few may have set up because they found it difficult to get a partnership (or even a job) with another firm. These sole practitioners are usually best avoided, although it should be emphasised that they are in a minority; most sole practitioners are fine.

- **Legal Aid Practices:** Several years ago, most firms did at least some Legal Aid work. However, with the development of the Community

Legal Service and the changes that have come in (for example, the fact that Legal Aid is no longer available for some areas of work), many firms have pulled out of Legal Aid work altogether. This inevitably means that those left will need to specialise more in this type of work. If you are on any sort of benefit or a very low income, you should (unless your case is one that can be dealt with on a no win no fee basis) look for one of these firms. They will have the Community Legal Service logo on their paper and advertising, or you can find them by the CLS website www.justask.org.uk. For further information about Legal Aid and the Community Legal Service, see the section above.

- 'Niche' practices: These are normally small firms or sole practitioners who specialise in just one or two areas of work. For example, some firms will just do employment work, immigration work or personal injury claims. If your problem falls within their area of expertise, they are usually an excellent choice as they will be very good and focused on what they do. However, sometimes a problem will fall within several categories, and in this case you may (but not always) be better going to a larger firm (such as a High Street firm) where they can deal with your problem 'in the round'. For example, some clients with employment claims, particularly if they involve stress at work or disability discrimination, will also have a claim against their employer for personal injury. It is often best if the same firm deals with both these claims so you should try to choose a firm that does both employment and personal injury work.

Lexcel

Lexcel is the Law Society's Quality Mark for solicitors. If a solicitors' firm displays the Lexcel logo, this means that they have been independently assessed as having achieved the Law Society's practice management standards.

Fat cats and dirty rats

Solicitors generally tend to have a bad press, and are frequently described disparagingly as 'fat cats' or worse, even by quite senior politicians who ought to know better. Although, of course, there are a few bad solicitors, there are bad eggs in every profession; the majority of solicitors are reasonably good, and often excellent. Perhaps the most common problem is that solicitors sometimes do not have very good 'people skills' and therefore, although they are in fact doing quite a good job, they do not explain things properly to their clients or come over as being pompous or uncaring. However, even if a solicitor *is* pompous and uncaring, this does not mean that he is not a good solicitor or that he is not dealing with your case properly. Solicitors have their professional pride and most of them try to do a good job for all their clients, even if they do not like them personally.

As regards the 'fat cats' charge, it is true that some firms, in particular firms in the City of London, do have very high charges and high incomes. However, these firms also have very high expenses and the solicitors usually have to work extremely long hours. Generally they are working for big companies who can well afford their fees, and as they are prepared to pay them they must feel that they are getting good value. The firms of solicitors who tend to act for the ordinary person are not able to charge such high fees. However, they still have many of the expenses (such as staff, indemnity insurance, IT costs, maintaining a legal library and training) of the larger firms. Some have financial difficulties. Many firms operate with large overdrafts. Indeed, one of the problems with Legal Aid work now is that the fees paid to solicitors are so low (there have only been a few fee increases in the past ten years) that they are unable to operate at a profit. This is one reason why so many firms of solicitors have withdrawn from Legal Aid work.

Why use a solicitor?

One of the results of the bad press on solicitors is that some people get the impression that it is better not to go to a solicitor at all, but to use someone unqualified. Here are some reasons why it is better to consult a solicitor:

- All solicitors have spent many years training before they are allowed to practise as a solicitor. Most of them will have a law degree; others will have passed a similar set of exams; all will then have done a year's additional studying, followed by a period of two years as a trainee solicitor. Some solicitors (such as former legal executives) will have followed a slightly different training pattern, but it will be equally rigorous.

- Even after qualification all solicitors now have to do a minimum of 16 hours per year 'continuing education', and have to certify every year when applying for their practising certificates that they have done so.

- All solicitors' firms carry professional indemnity insurance. This is a condition of being allowed to practise as a solicitor and must be proved to the Law Society when applying for the firm's solicitors' practising certificates. This means that if you have a valid claim against a solicitor you can be confident that it will be paid.

- All solicitors also contribute to the Compensation Fund which will make payments to clients if a claim cannot be made under a solicitor's indemnity insurance policy. For example, this may be the case where a solicitor has been dishonest.

- There are special procedures you can use to get your solicitors' bill reduced if you are overcharged (see below). These are not available if legal work is done by someone who is not a member of a firm of solicitors, for example, if a bank is appointed as executor of a will rather than a solicitor.

- Solicitors operate under a code of ethics. If they break this, a complaint can be made against them and, ultimately, if the complaint is upheld, they can lose their right to practise as a solicitor.

- Because of their long training and practice within the law, solicitors develop a 'feel' for the way things operate within the legal system. Also, their training and work teach them to analyse problems. They can all usually give some useful advice at least, even if your problem does not fall within their field of practice.

But do not expect too much

Sometimes people have unrealistic expectations from solicitors. You should note the following:

- Although, as stated above, all solicitors have a general 'feel' for legal problems, you must realise that nowadays most solicitors specialise, and will not generally be prepared to give advice (other than very general advice) outside their area of expertise. So although all solicitors will be able to tell you something helpful, only someone who practises in the correct area of law will be able to answer your question. You need therefore to do some research before consulting solicitors to find the best person for your problem.

- Solicitors deal with legal problems; do not expect them to act as psychologists or social workers.

- Solicitors are not banks and you cannot expect them to make payments on your behalf, effectively loaning you money. You will be expected to pay all expenses connected with your case promptly, in advance, unless of course it has been specifically agreed between you and the solicitors before they start the work that they will fund certain expenses.

- Solicitors are running a business not a charity, and will expect to be paid for their work. Do not expect them to work for free or for minimal payment.

- Most types of legal work take time. With the best will in the world, it is often difficult if not impossible for your solicitor to speed things up. Delays will not usually be his fault as he will be waiting for other people to respond, e.g. with reports (such as medical reports in personal injury claims), searches (such as local searches in conveyancing) and replies from other firms of solicitors (who in turn may be unable to respond until they hear from their clients). It will normally be beyond the power of your solicitor to do anything about these delays other than write reminder letters.

- Litigation in particular is unpredictable. You may feel certain that you have a good case but bear in mind that the Judge might not agree with you. Listen to your solicitor's advice and do not immediately assume, if he suggests that you settle the case, that he is being negative. All litigation solicitors know of cases that appeared virtually certain to win - until they got to court. It is always better to settle if you can. Even if you do not get all that you want, this is much better than losing everything (and having to pay your opponent's costs as well as your own). However, this does not mean that you should roll over and allow your opponent to trample all over you. It is a question of balance. A good solicitor will fight for his client to achieve the best deal.

- Solicitors are busy people and have a large caseload. Unless your case is extremely urgent (and your idea of what is urgent and the solicitors' may differ), you will have to wait for your case to take its turn.

Remember that they have a duty to their other clients and can only do one thing at a time.

- Finally, bear in mind that for some problems there won't be anything your solicitor (or indeed any solicitor) can realistically do to help you.

An ethical profession

Although solicitors do not take an oath, such as the Hippocratic oath of doctors, they do have a code of ethics that underpins the profession and affects the way that they practise. They are also bound by various other rules and statutory regulations that are together set out in a rather formidable book called 'The Guide to the Professional Conduct of Solicitors' (which can now be found online at the Law Society's website at **www.guide-online.lawsociety.org.uk**). All of these rules and regulations are perhaps summarised by Rule 1, which sets out the basic principles of the profession:

A Solicitor shall not do anything in the course of practising as a solicitor, or permit another person to do anything on his or her behalf, which compromises or impairs or is likely to compromise or impair any of the following:

(a) The solicitor's independence or integrity

(b) A person's freedom to instruct a solicitor of his or her choice

(c) The solicitor's duty to act in the best interests of the client

(d) The good repute of the solicitor or of the solicitor's profession

(e) The solicitor's proper standard of work

(f) The solicitor's duty to the court

The professional rules are under review at the time of writing, but it is unlikely that these fundamental principals will be substantially altered.

Solicitors' charges

One of the first things that people think about when considering instructing a solicitor is 'how much will it cost?' Solicitors can be expensive but it is easy to forget this and run up a large bill. The solicitors' rules now specify that they should tell you in advance what the work is likely to cost and subsequently tell you if their costs are going to exceed this. It might be helpful here to run through the various charging methods used by solicitors.

- **Charging by the hour:** This is the most common method of charging and probably the least popular with clients. However, sometimes it is difficult to see how solicitors can be paid fairly any other way. For example, with litigation it is impossible to know at the beginning whether a case will settle after a few weeks or run on for years and turn into an expensive trial.

All fee earners are allocated an hourly rate by their firm (which varies according to their status and experience) and they will charge on this basis. Sometimes they will reserve the right to charge uplift on this (generally 50 per cent), for example, if the work they have done is unusually complex or urgent.

The charging rates charged by solicitors may seem high to you, but remember that it has to cover all the firm's expenses, such as staff salaries, premises expenses, IT and library expenses, continuing education, insurance, etc. It is not just in respect of that solicitor's own salary!

The majority of solicitors will time record as they work, on time sheets, and this data is then fed into a computer. For the purpose of time recording, time is divided into units, usually of six minutes each, so this is the minimum time that will be entered whenever they do any work on your case. Standard telephone calls and letters are generally entered as one unit each. So if your solicitor's hourly rate is £120, each time you ring him to ask how your case is coming on will cost you a minimum of £12. Time recording is the standard method of charging which will be used if no other fee structure is specified.

- **Fixed fees:** This method is often used when the solicitor knows from the start the amount of work involved in a case. It is obviously preferable from the client's point of view, as they know where they stand and can budget properly. It is most commonly used in conveyancing and debt collecting work, and for straightforward drafting jobs such as wills and tenancy agreements. However, solicitors are sometimes willing to agree a fixed fee for other work and it is often worth asking a solicitor if they would be prepared to act for you on a fixed fee basis.

- **No-win no-fee:** Until fairly recently this concept was anathema to the profession as it was felt improper for a solicitor to have a financial stake in the success or failure of the litigation he was conducting. Until 1995, this policy was not permitted for litigation work.

However, it is now being encouraged and is viewed by the Government as a replacement for Legal Aid for some types of case. There are two types of no-win no-fee - conditional fee agreements and contingency agreements.

- **Conditional fees:** This is the only type of no-win no-fee agreement permitted for litigation work. Under these agreements, a solicitor will still charge on a time costing basis. However, he will only get paid if the case is won, when, because he has taken the risk of losing his fees, he will be paid a success fee which will normally be an 'uplift' on his fees of an agreed percentage. The percentage will depend upon the risk taken by the solicitor in bringing the case but must not be more than 100 per cent.

Because an unsuccessful litigant is usually responsible for his opponent's costs, conditional fee agreements must be backed by an insurance policy that will cover these fees in the event of the case being lost, together with any disbursements incurred. As most conditional fee agreements relate to personal injury claims it is important that there is provision for disbursements to be paid, as medical reports can be very expensive. There will also be other expenses such as court fees.

Before acting on a conditional fee basis, your solicitor will require you to sign a form of agreement. These are extremely long; you should make sure that you understand it properly before signing.

Further information on conditional fee agreements can be found in David Marshall's article in Part 3.

- **Contingency fees:** This is where, instead of charging on a time costing basis, the solicitor receives as his fee a percentage of the award. This type of agreement is not allowed for County Court and High Court litigation. However, it is permissible for claims to the Employment Tribunal (which for some reason are not defined as 'litigation'). Some firms are now starting to charge on this basis for Employment Tribunal claims. The standard percentage is 30 per cent.

Because winning parties in Employment Tribunal claims are not generally awarded costs (i.e. the loser does not normally pay the winner's legal costs), and because there are frequently no disbursements involved, the form of agreement used by solicitors for this work is generally shorter than the contingency fee agreement used for County Court and High Court work. However, it is still quite a complex document and you should be sure that you understand it before signing. For example, it will probably provide for you to pay the solicitor on a time costing basis for any work done if you decide not to proceed with your claim.

- **Legal Aid/The Community Legal Service:** If you are on a low income (generally if you are on benefit of some kind), you will normally be eligible for some advice and perhaps more specialist help from solicitors who are part of the Community Legal Service. Legal Aid is becoming less important now as fewer people qualify on financial grounds and some types of work (e.g. personal injury work) are no longer covered. The Community Legal Service is discussed in more detail above.

How to minimise or control your solicitor's costs

Here are some tips on how to minimise the costs that you pay:

- Do your own research before consulting a solicitor. This book will help you. If you understand your problem and have some familiarity with the area of law involved, you will understand the solicitor better and he will have to spend less time explaining basic legal concepts to you.

- Make sure your papers are in order before handing them over. Put correspondence and other documentation into chronological order - this will be a great help to your solicitor and will enable him to get a grip on your case earlier. He will also be grateful to you for saving him from a boring job. If he has to sort out the papers himself, he will of course charge you for his time for doing this, which (if the bundle of papers is a large one) could work out quite expensive for you.

- Make sure that you are quite clear about your solicitor's charges before you agree to let him handle your case. Do not be afraid of speaking out about this at your first meeting with him. In fact, if your solicitor does not give you clear information about how he proposes to charge, you should seriously consider going to another firm.

- If the type of work involved is not suitable for a fixed fee and the solicitor is going to charge on a time costing basis, you can always stipulate a maximum amount which the solicitor cannot exceed without your permission (make sure this is put in writing).

- You can also ask your solicitor to invoice you regularly, for example, monthly. This is a good idea as it will spread out the cost, and you will not be presented with a large bill at the end of the case which you may find hard to pay.

- All solicitors are now obliged to send a 'client care' letter to new clients giving information about their proposed charges, the name and status of the fee earner dealing with your case, and details of the firm's complaints procedure. Make sure you read this letter, particularly the section regarding the solicitors' fees, and make sure that this agrees with what was discussed with you. For example, if your solicitor has agreed not to exceed £500 without your permission, check that this is mentioned in the letter. If not, write back setting out what was agreed and stating that your instructions are conditional upon this.

- Although a timely reminder now and again is a good idea, do not pester your solicitor, for example, by ringing him up several times a day. Remember that if he is charging on a time costing basis you will be charged for every call that you make.

- You should always assist your solicitor in every way you can. If he requests information or documents from you, these should be sent as soon as possible. If you delay, you could prejudice your case. For example, in litigation matters, there are strict time limits for disclosing documents in a case. If you do not disclose a document in time, you may not be able to use it at trial. Remember, if a solicitor has to keep writing to you requesting information, you will be charged for this work.

- Listen to your solicitor's advice. For example, if he considers that your claim is not a strong one, think very carefully before proceeding. He is probably right. If you do not agree and want to proceed, consider taking a second opinion first.

- When you receive your bill from your solicitor, check that it agrees with the figures set out in the client care letter or any subsequent costs letter. If it is for more than was agreed, write to your solicitor referring to the relevant letter and ask for the bill to be reduced to the agreed sum.

• If you are unhappy about the service you have received from your solicitors or the charge that they have made, write and complain. If your complaint is a valid one, they will usually agree to reduce their fee. See further on this below.

How to get good service

This is not the same as keeping your costs down, although many of the points below are very similar to those set out above.

• Make sure you choose the right solicitor for the job, ideally someone who specialises in the type of work you want him to do. Although he may seem more expensive, he will probably work out cheaper in the long run, particularly if he is charging on a time costing basis, as he will be able to work quicker due to his familiarity with the type of work and the fact that he has to do less research.

• Always pay promptly all bills and requests for money on account of costs (provided of course that they are reasonable).

• Give clear instructions to the solicitor. For example, make sure your paperwork is in order (preferably sorted in date order) and that you have provided him with everything he needs. Do not withhold any relevant information or tell any lies (if he finds that you have been lying to him he will probably be entitled to stop acting for you). In complex cases, clear (preferably typewritten) summaries and chronologies may be helpful.

• Always cooperate with your solicitor when asked, and provide any extra information he asks for promptly.

• Be pleasant and courteous to both your solicitor and his staff. He will not be pleased, for example, if he finds that you have reduced his secretary to tears because he or she was unable to provide you with information you wanted.

• Be reasonable - do not ring your solicitor up constantly (which will irritate him), or demand that he see you or deal with your case immediately. Remember that he has other clients as well and cannot always give your case preference.

• Consider writing to thank your solicitor at the conclusion of the matter, if you think he has done a particularly good job. Solicitors are only human after all!

Changing solicitors

If you are unhappy about the service provided by your solicitor, it is always open to you to take your work to another firm. In fact, if you have lost confidence in your solicitor or there has been a breakdown in communications, this is probably a good idea. However, if you simply have a feeling of unease about how your case is being handled, it might be best to take a second opinion first (perhaps from your local CAB or one of the free advice agencies on the internet) - your fears may be groundless. You should, in any event, first try to resolve any problems with your solicitor direct, at least as far as ongoing work is concerned, before going elsewhere.

If you do decide to change solicitors while a matter is ongoing, remember that your solicitor is entitled to retain your paperwork until you have paid all outstanding bills due to the firm. All solicitors can do this - it is called the solicitors' lien. This may cause you problems if you want to challenge the bill, for example, by obtaining a Law Society remuneration certificate. In this case, you would have to pay the bill in full but state in your covering letter that the payment was being made without prejudice to your right to ask for a remuneration certificate, and solely to allow the release of the paperwork. Your new solicitor will advise you and write this letter for you.

Changing solicitors during the course of a case should not be done lightly. The majority of solicitors are dealing perfectly competently with their client's work. Bear in mind, also, that your new solicitor will have to replicate some of the work of your earlier solicitor in order to familiarise himself with your case, so you may end up paying twice for the same work.

Complaints about solicitors' services and charges

You first need to decide which of the following categories your complaint falls under. Have your solicitors:

(1)   overcharged you or failed to calculate your bill properly;

(2)   provided a poor level of service and/or breached the solicitors' professional rules; or

(3)   been negligent or dishonest in the handling of your case?

These cases need to be dealt with differently.

(1) Overcharging

If you think that you have been overcharged, you should first of all write to your solicitors asking them to reduce your bill, and explaining why. If the person dealing with your case is unhelpful, your letter should be addressed to the firm's complaints partner and state that you are invoking their complaints procedure. You should find the name of the complaints partner in your client care letter; alternatively, you can ring the firm up and ask for the name of the complaints partner or the person to whom formal complaints against the firm should be sent. Your letter should state that you require a reply within a short period of time, say seven days. Be careful about time, as if you are going to ask for a remuneration certificate, this must be done within one month of receiving notice from the solicitors.

If an appeal to your solicitors is unsuccessful you should proceed as follows:

Remuneration Certificates: For all work which did not involve court proceedings, you can require the firm to obtain a remuneration certificate from the Law Society. Under this procedure, the Law Society will check your bill and decide whether it is fair or not. If the bill is found to be unfair, they will substitute a lower fee. Solicitors must give you notice of your right to do this (and are unable to issue legal proceedings against you for unpaid fees until they have done so). Notice is now generally given on the invoice itself, often in small type on the back of the bill.

If you wish your invoice to be checked in this way, you must tell the solicitors within one month of the notice being served on you. You must also pay half the fee, all of the VAT and any outstanding disbursements, although in exceptional circumstances this requirement can be waived. If you wish for a waiver, you should contact the Office for the Supervision of Solicitors at 8 Dormer Place, Leamington Spa, Warwickshire, CV32 5AE (although make sure you get your request for a remuneration certificate to your solicitors within the one month period - tell them that you are applying for waiver). When you make the payment, you should say that you are only doing this on condition the solicitors apply for a remuneration certificate.

Remember that if you pay your bill in full, you lose the right to a remuneration certificate.

Once you have notified your solicitors that you require a remuneration certificate, they will obtain the form, complete it and send it to you for your comments. You should then send the form back to the solicitors and they will send it, together with the file, to the Law Society. The solicitors must do the actual application to the Law Society - you cannot do this.

When the Law Society receives the papers, they will initially try to conciliate between you and the solicitors' firm. If this does not succeed, they will then prepare a report and send both you and the solicitors a provisional assessment saying what fee they think is fair. If either you or the solicitor do not agree with this, they will then issue a remuneration certificate for the amount that you have to pay. If you do not agree with this you can appeal, but this must be within 28 days.

Assessment (formerly known as taxation) by the Court: If your case has involved any court proceedings, a remuneration certificate is not available. However, you can have your solicitor's charges reviewed by the court. This used to be known (rather confusingly) as 'taxation'; however, it is now called 'assessment'.

Court assessment of bills is a somewhat complex process and it would be best to get some advice, at least, before taking any action. You need to request the assessment within one month of having the bill sent to you. If you request it later, you run the risk of the court refusing to allow the assessment, particularly if you have not paid your bill. You lose your right to assessment after a year.

Once you have requested an assessment of your solicitors' bill, they will (assuming that they are unable to negotiate an agreement with you) have to have a special bill of costs drawn up giving full details of how the bill has been calculated. This will then be sent to you and you will have to specify which parts you object to and why. At this stage, you will probably need some advice.

To get advice on solicitor's costs, it is perhaps best to speak initially to a Law Costs Draftsman. These are specialists whose job is the drawing up of solicitors' bills for court assessments and representing solicitors on those bills at court. They are the best people to advise you whether you have a chance of getting your solicitors' bill reduced. Although their instructions normally come from solicitors, they will generally agree to advise members of the public direct on 'solicitor and own client' assessments. However, they will not normally represent you at any court hearing other than through solicitors. You will either have to represent yourself, or instruct another firm of solicitors.

As with all court proceedings, the winner is entitled to have his costs paid by the loser. Be warned that, in the case of assessments, if the bill is reduced by less than 20 per cent (and particularly if it is not reduced at all), you will almost certainly face an order that you pay your former solicitors' costs. This could be quite expensive, as you will have to pay not only all court fees, but also their expenses of having the bill of costs drawn up and the cost of their attendance at court.

To find a Law Costs draftsman in your area contact:

The Association of Law Costs Draftsmen

SOC www.alcd.org.uk

Mrs Chapman, Tel: 01279 741 404

Or look in Yellow Pages under Legal Services.

(2) Poor service

<u>The solicitors' own complaints procedure</u>

If you feel that you have had a poor service from your solicitors, you should first of all use the firm's own complaints procedure. Your complaint should be addressed to the firm's complaint's partner. This can be done by a telephone call, in which case you should keep a written note of your conversation. However, it is best to make your complaint by letter, as there is then a written record.

You should draft this letter with some care. Make sure you give your name and address, the firm's reference and the name of the solicitor or other fee earner who acted for you. The letter should be dated. Set out your problem clearly but keep your letter as short and concise as possible, giving any relevant dates. If possible, give examples of the problems. You should say whether you want your complaint to be dealt with in writing or whether you would like a meeting. As with all letters of this type, you should use short paragraphs and bullet points and, if it is not possible to have the letter typed, make sure that your handwriting is legible. The letter should be addressed to the Complaints Handling Partner (if you do not know his name) and marked 'Private and Confidential'.

You should receive a reply within 14 days, but it may take a little longer if your problem is a complex one. If you have not had a response within, say 28 days, or if you are unable to resolve your problem with your solicitors direct, you should then consider going to the Office for the Supervision of Solicitors.

Your solicitors should not charge you for their time in dealing with a complaint under their complaints procedure. If they send you a bill for this work, you should refuse to pay it and report them to the Office for the Supervision of Solicitors.

Complaining to the Office for the Supervision of Solicitors ('OSS')

The OSS was set up by the Law Society and is funded by them. However, it is independent in that the Law Society cannot get involved in individual disputes. Its task is to deal with complaints about solicitors and to regulate their work. It is governed by a mixture of solicitors and members of the public, appointed by the Master of the Rolls.

If you have not been able to resolve your complaint satisfactorily through your solicitor's own complaints procedure, you can then complain to the OSS. However, be sure to make your complaint within six months of your complaint to your solicitors or the OSS may refuse to consider it. You may wish first to contact the OSS helpline on 0845 608 6565. They can give you some initial advice and send you a form. You can also follow the link to the OSS from the Law Society website (the link is under 'visitors' on the right hand side) for information about the OSS and their service. You can also download the form.

Office for the Supervision of Solicitors

www.lawsociety.org.uk

Victoria Court
8 Dormer Place
Leamington Spa

Warwickshire CV32 5AE
Helpline: 0845 608 6565
Email: enquiries@lawsociety.org.uk

The OSS will first contact the solicitors and get their response to your complaint. They may, at that stage, decide not to take it any further. If so, they will write and tell you why. If they consider your complaint a valid one and are not able to negotiate an agreement between you and the solicitors, they will investigate and make a report. Both you and the solicitor will have an opportunity to comment on this. If your case is a complex one, they will sometimes visit you to discuss the case. A member of the OSS adjudication team will then make a decision.

The OSS aims to deal with 90 per cent of complaints made to them within a three-month period and the rest within a five-month period. However, there have been problems at the OSS in the past and frequently serious delays have taken place. Recently, though, this situation has improved and it is probable that your complaint will be dealt with within the five-month period.

If the OSS finds that your solicitors' service was not good enough they can do the following:

- reduce your solicitor's bill;

- order the solicitor to pay you compensation of up to £5,000;

- tell the solicitor to correct any mistake and pay any costs involved.

If your complaint is one of professional misconduct, the OSS will not normally make a financial order. However, they can refer the matter to the Solicitors' Disciplinary Tribunal for disciplinary action against the solicitor and any findings will remain on his record throughout his professional life.

Solicitors' Disciplinary Tribunal

If the decision reached by the OSS involves action from the solicitor, e.g. a payment of compensation to you, the solicitor must do this within the time laid down in the decision. If they fail to comply with an OSS decision, then this is professional misconduct and the OSS will bring a complaint against the solicitor/solicitors' firm to the Solicitors'

Disciplinary Tribunal, who have the power to fine the solicitor, suspend the solicitor from practice, or ultimately take away his practising certificate altogether. Alternatively, the OSS may consider that the solicitor's conduct is so reprehensible that they have no alternative but to refer the matter direct to the Solicitors' Disciplinary Tribunal from the start. This is normally done where the solicitor is suspected of dishonesty or mishandling client's money. The Solicitors' Disciplinary Tribunal is independent and holds public hearings. Their decisions are often reported in the local press.

<u>The Legal Services Ombudsman</u>

If you have a complaint about the way your claim has been dealt with by the OSS, you can complain about them to the Legal Services Ombudsman, currently Ann Abraham. This must be done within three months of the OSS closing their file. If the Ombudsman does not agree with the decision reached by the OSS she cannot substitute her conclusions for those of the OSS; however, she can ask them to reconsider their decision (which they will then do).

Office of the Legal Services Ombudsman

OFF   www.olso.org

22 Oxford Court
Oxford Street
Manchester M2 3WQ
Lo-call number: 0845 601 0794
Tel: 0161 236 9532
Fax: 0161 236 2651
Email: enquiries.olso@gtnet.gov.uk

(3) Negligent or dishonest solicitors

If you consider that your solicitor has been negligent in the way he has handled your case, you may have a claim against him for compensation, for example, if you have lost money or have spent money trying to put things right. All solicitors are covered by professional indemnity insurance so if you have a valid claim, you can be sure it will be paid.

Under contract law, your claim will be for compensation to put you in the (financial) position you would have been in had the solicitor not acted negligently. For example, if your County Court claim has been 'struck out' (discontinued by the court) because the solicitors missed a deadline, the court will have to assess what award would have been made to you, and the solicitors will have to pay this sum to you, plus any legal costs incurred by you in bringing the claim.

If you contact the OSS about your problem they will, if appropriate, refer you to a solicitor local to you who is on their negligence panel. This solicitor will give you an hour's free advice and will let you know whether, in his opinion, your solicitors have been negligent. If he thinks that they have, he will advise you how to proceed.

Although there is no reason why you should not act in person, particularly for a simple claim, for more complex matters it is probably best to be represented by a firm of solicitors. If your claim is successful, you will get your legal costs paid. If your case is a good one, you may be able to persuade another firm to act for you on the basis that they will get paid at the conclusion of the case, although you will probably have to pay any disbursements.

Solicitors are generally quite happy about suing other firms of solicitors (the fees they will get from the case usually overcome any reluctance they may have in bringing a claim against one of their brethren!). However, they may be reluctant to take a claim on if they know the solicitor personally. You may feel happier, therefore, consulting a firm of solicitors in a different town.

If your solicitor has been dishonest, generally you can make a claim against his firm in the same way and they will be covered by their professional indemnity insurance. However, if the solicitor is a sole practitioner, or if all of the partners in the firm were involved in the dishonest conduct, this may not be possible and you may have to make a claim instead to the compensation fund. This is run by the OSS and you can contact them for details.

Further information about solicitors

The Law Society

SOC www.lawsociety.org.uk .he Law Society

The Law Society is the solicitor's professional body and it performs many functions. It regulates solicitors and enforces this via the Office for the Supervision of Solicitors. It also, in separate departments, gives advice and support to solicitors and acts as their 'trade union'. On another front, it advises the Government on legal matters, in particular on proposed legislation, and will lobby government on matters it thinks important. In this role, it tries to promote the interests of the general public as well as those of solicitors, and will often work in cooperation with consumer organisations.

The Law Society has a fairly comprehensive website that has much useful information about its services and legal matters generally (although finding information on particular topics is not always straightforward - do not give up if you cannot find what you want immediately!). Linked to this is the excellent 'Solicitors Online' directory of solicitors, which is discussed below.

Apart from this, the only services offered directly to the public are careers advice, location of solicitors and their firms (through the Records department), and the Office for the Supervision of Solicitors.

The Law Society is based in Chancery Lane in London, with offices also at Leamington Spa and Redditch. However, any enquiries can initially be made to the Chancery Lane address.

The Law Society
113 Chancery Lane
London WC2A 1PL
Tel: 020 7242 1222
Fax: 020 7831 0344

How to find & choose a solicitor

Choosing a solicitor is an important matter. Before doing anything, you should think about the sort of solicitor you want. For example, do you want:

- a local solicitor;
- a solicitor who is a specialist in a particular area of law;

- a firm of solicitors who offer Legal Aid;
- a firm that offers no-win no-fee agreements;
- a firm that offers disabled access or home visits;
- a solicitor of the same sex as you;
- a firm of solicitors who will correspond with you by email;
- a cheap, cost-effective, or a 'Rolls Royce' service.

There are many ways of locating a good solicitor, so you should avoid using a service that charges you for a referral to a solicitor. Here are some suggestions:

Personal recommendation

As always, this is probably one of the best ways of finding a good solicitor. Ask around your friends and relatives about the solicitors they have used in the past. Remember, however, that solicitors specialise and, for example, a good matrimonial solicitor will not normally be able to help you with your boundary dispute.

Referral

There are many free advice organisations that can help you find a solicitor. Some of them may have a panel of solicitors who specialise in a particular area of law, e.g. employment law, which you can be referred to for a free interview or fixed fee, for example, the OSS panel of solicitors who advise on solicitors' negligence mentioned above. Often a very good source of information about local solicitors is your local CAB. For further information about specialist referrals, see the individual legal sections below. Beware of commercial organisations that make referrals to solicitors for personal injury work (such as some who advertise on the television) as they will usually make a charge for their referral if you win your claim, which you will have to pay on top of the solicitors' fees.

Solicitors' panels and accreditation schemes

For some areas of law and practice there are specialist solicitor panels. To join these, the solicitor will often have to pass a written examination and/or have extensive practical experience in the area of work concerned. Some of these schemes also admit, or are intended for, non-solicitors.

When choosing a solicitor in these areas of law, unless you know something about the solicitor concerned (and many excellent specialist solicitors are not panel members), it is often a good idea to choose a panel member as you can then be sure that the solicitor will have sufficient knowledge and experience.

At present the following panels are in operation:

- Children panel (family law solicitors who specialise in work regarding children)
- Clinical negligence panel (solicitors who specialise in the highly technical field of medical negligence - claims against doctors and hospitals)
- Family law panel (solicitors and legal executives who specialise in family/matrimonial work)
- Immigration law panel (solicitors, legal executives and paralegals who specialise in immigration work)
- Licensing of insolvency practitioners (solicitors wishing to practise as insolvency practitioners must be licensed)
- Mental health review panel (solicitors, legal executives and paralegals who provide representation for patients before the Mental Health Review Tribunal)
- Personal injury panel (solicitors and legal executives who specialise in personal injury work. All accident line solicitors must be members of the personal injury panel)
- Planning panel (solicitors who specialise in planning law)

Further information about these panels are, where relevant, given in the individual law sections in Part 3. You can also find further information about them on the Law Society's website - follow the 'specialist panel's' link on **www.solicitors-online.com**.

Law Society Directories

The Law Society print quite detailed regional directories of solicitors which are generally available in CABs and public libraries. These will give details of the type of work the firm will do and whether they do Legal Aid work or not. Do not assume always, however, that because a firm says it does a certain type of work, for example, insolvency work, that they actually employ a specialist in that field.

For help in finding a specialist solicitor, you can also telephone:

The Law Society: 020 7242 1222

Solicitors Online

SOC
REC www.solicitors-online.com

The Law Society also operate an excellent website, Solicitors Online which has up to date details (or as up to date as the Law Society's records) of all firms of solicitors, and the areas of work done by each firm, together with other information such as whether they do legal aid work or have access for the disabled. You can also see details of the solicitors working at the firm, such as when they qualified and whether they belong to any specialist panels. If the firm has a website there will be a link to it. Finally, if you decide to use them, you can print out a map showing you how to find their office. You can use the search facilities on the site not only to locate a suitable firm, but also to find an individual solicitor (provided you can spell their name correctly). If you have internet access, using Solicitors Online should be your starting point for finding a solicitor.

Other Directories

Just Ask directory

OFF
REC www.justask.org.uk

The Legal Services Commission, which is the organisation that administers what used to be called the Legal Aid Scheme but which is now called the Community Legal Service, publish a directory of all organisations, including solicitors, who are part of the Community Legal Service. This directory can be found at advice centres, local libraries and CABs. The Commission also have an extensive website, called Just Ask, which you can use to find solicitors (and other advice agencies) by area and by type of law.

Yellow Pages

This is a very popular way of locating a local solicitor. Most firms will have a display ad which will give information about the type of work that they do and whether they do legal aid work or not.

Other internet sources

There are several directories of solicitors' firms on the internet. The most comprehensive is the Law Society's Solicitors Online site discussed above. If you are looking specifically for a firm of solicitors who have a website and, by implication, can communicate with you by email, the best place to start is probably Delia Venables' site. She also gives a list of solicitors who are prepared to give free initial advice by email. For more information on Delia's site and Infolaw, see the section on the internet in Part 1. Also set out below are a number of commercial sites that will help you find a solicitor.

Delia Venables

com www.venables.co.uk

REC Follow the link to Free Legal Information for Individuals.

Infolaw

com www.infolaw.co.uk

REC Another list of lawyers on the internet can be found on a site maintained by Nick Holmes - follow the link for lawyers' listings.

Lawjunction

COM www.lawjunction.co.uk

This is a site where potential clients can submit details of their problem, and solicitors on their panel will give a quote on how much they would charge to do the work. The client can choose which firm it instructs (or can decide not to instruct any). It is a free service at the time of writing.

In general, you should be wary, however, of referrals by commercial 'portal' sites (including some in this book, which are included for their free content), as the solicitors on their panel may not have been checked out by the referring organisation in any detail. Also they may not have a panel solicitor in your area. It is generally best to locate a solicitor by one of the other methods discussed above.

Logos associated with solicitors' firms

There are many 'quality marks' which can be obtained by solicitors and which you may see on their headed paper and in their advertisements. The most common are set out below:

 CLS logo: Organisations showing this logo have obtained the Community Legal Service Quality Mark.

 CDS logo: Solicitors showing this logo have a contract with the Legal Services Commission to do criminal defence work.

 Legal Aid logo: This is the old logo indicating that a firm does Legal Aid work. It has now been superseded by the CLS logo above although it is still used by some firms.

 Legal Aid Franchise logo: This is the old logo that solicitors could use if they had obtained a Legal Aid franchise. Again this logo has now been superseded by the CLS logo above.

 Lexcel logo: Solicitors showing this logo have obtained the Law Society's Lexcel Quality Mark.

 Family Law logo: Solicitors who are members of the Family Law Panel all specialise in family/matrimonial work.

 SFLA logo: Solicitors displaying this logo are members of the Solicitors Family Law Association. Membership is related to the individual rather than to the firm.

 Children logo: Solicitors in the Children panel will all be experienced in legal work involving children, particularly care proceedings.

 Accident Line logo: Solicitors displaying this logo are participating in the Law Society's Accident Line scheme for personal injury claims.

 Transaction logo: Solicitors displaying this logo have agreed to adopt the Law Society's national transaction protocol in conveyancing matters.

 Lawyers for your Business: Solicitors' firms who display this logo are participants in the Lawyers for your Business scheme administered by the Law Society.

 Investors in People logo: Solicitors displaying this logo have obtained the Investors in People standard.

 ISO 9001 logo: Solicitors displaying this logo have obtained the ISO 9001 standard.

Licensed Conveyancers

The licensed conveyancers profession is a new profession. It started in May 1987 when the Council for Licensed Conveyancers - the body that regulates the profession - issued the first licences. All licensed conveyancers have to undergo training and pass the examinations set by the Council. Once they have obtained their full licence they are allowed to offer conveyancing services direct to the public (a service which formerly could only be done by solicitors) and practise either as a sole principal or in partnership.

Many licensed conveyancers work in solicitors' firms. However, there are also many firms of licensed conveyancers and these are a good alternative to using a solicitor for conveyancing work. If you want to find a licensed conveyancer, you can contact the Council who will let you have a list of licensed conveyancers in practice in your area. You may also be able to get this information from your local CAB or Housing Information Centre. You can also find them via the Yellow Pages but be careful to ensure that the Council does license the person you use. You can always telephone the Council to check before you use them.

If you have any complaint against a licensed conveyancer that has not been satisfactorily resolved through their complaints system, you can contact the Council at the address below.

The Council for Licensed Conveyancers

SOC www.theclc.gov.uk

16 Glebe Road
Chelmsford
Essex CN1 1QG
Tel: 01245 349 599
Fax: 01245 341 300
Email: clc@conveyancer.org.uk

Barristers

Barristers (also called Counsel - the same word is used for both singular and plural) are a different profession to solicitors. Their training is somewhat different and there are fewer of them. Barristers tend to be the 'specialists' of the legal profession. The public cannot normally instruct them direct, and anyone wishing to consult them will have to do so via a solicitor. They have two main functions: to provide specialist advice and drafting services to solicitors, and to provide advocacy services. Apart from a few solicitors with the Higher Rights of Audience certificate, only barristers can represent clients in the higher courts. Often they will both advise and represent a client in litigation.

Barristers (when practising as a barrister, many of them will work as employed lawyers with large organisations) must be self-employed. However, they tend to practise together in 'chambers' or 'sets', where they all share accommodation costs, and one or more clerks who do all the administrative work. The majority of barristers practise in London, mostly in the Inns of Court - the Inner Temple, Middle Temple, Lincoln's Inn and Grays Inn. There are also many thriving chambers in the provinces. The majority of the senior and more eminent barristers, though, practise in London. More information about barristers can be found on the Bar Council website.

Apart from the Bar Pro Bono Unit (see above), the only way, realistically, the general public can get advice from a barrister without going through a solicitor is by getting information from their websites. A full list of these can be found on Delia Venables' website (follow the link to services for Lawyers). Most barristers' websites are aimed at solicitors and other lawyers, and the information contained is often heavy-going if you are not legally trained (and sometimes even if you are!). Some of the more consumer-orientated barristers' websites are included in Part 3.

The Bar Council

SOC www.barcouncil.org.uk

This site has information about barristers and the work that they do. Also, it provides details on how to complain about a barrister.

Paying for unqualified legal advice

There are many organisations that offer legal advice and assistance of one sort or another for a fee, but whose members do not have a professional qualification. Perhaps those most normally encountered by the general public are will-writing companies. However, there are others, for example, employment law consultants. These organisations are often very good.

However, you need to be wary when using them. If the advisors do not have a professional qualification, their knowledge and experience may not be as good as that of, say, a solicitor. A short course on, for example, writing wills cannot equate to the long training received by a solicitor, which will give him a greater depth and all-round knowledge, and enable him to identify and deal with problems better 'in the round'.

Also, when instructing these firms, you need to consider what courses of action are open to you if things go wrong. Are they a member of a professional organisation? Do they have a complaints system and professional indemnity insurance? If not, you should be very wary about using them.

Part 3

Specific Areas of Law

Specific areas of law

This section looks at specific areas of law. For each area, there is some general comment (particularly for the areas of law most commonly encountered by the general public), followed by various sources of further information. Large areas of law and practice may be divided into sub-sections. Each section is dealt with differently.

However, the sources of information given in the sections are generally specific to the area of law concerned. The following websites can generally give assistance or can be used to find advice for all areas of law, and are therefore given here so it is not necessary to repeat them continually in the individual sections:

Adviceguide

**OFF
REC**
www.adviceguide.org.uk
This is the excellent guide provided by the National Association of Citizens Advice Bureaux. Advice is provided on many topics, from abortion to the Youth Court. There is also a separate section for Scotland. Highly recommended.

Just Ask

**OFF
REC**
www.justask.org.uk
This is the website provided by the Legal Services Commission (formerly the Legal Aid Board). You can use it to find an organisation within the Community Legal Partnership (i.e. one which will provide free information to those on benefit or a low income). See Part 1 on the CLS for further details. There is also a directory which you can find in local libraries, CABs and advice centres. Also, there is the

CLS Call Centre
Tel: 0845 608 1122
Minicom: 0845 609 6677
This can be used to find your local CLS advisors.

Solicitors Online

**OFF
REC**
www.solicitors-online.com
This is the online directory maintained by the Law Society that you can use to find a solicitor near you. It also has basic information

about solicitors' firms and the work that they do.

UK Online

GOV
REC www.ukonline.gov.uk

This is the government site that you can use to find information about government services and departments. You can also find further information on various 'life episodes' such as dealing with crime, or death and bereavement. The site has excellent links to outside services that can give help and information.

Delia Venables

COM
REC www.venables.co.uk

Delia Venables maintains an excellent series of pages with internet links to all types of legal sites. It is impossible for any printed book to be completely up to date. Visit Delia's site to find all the latest legal websites, in particular visit the 'New on the legal internet' section. See further on Delia's site in Part I.

The Court Service

GOV
REC www.courtservice.gov.uk

The Court Service publishes a number of very helpful leaflets to assist people wishing to bring legal proceedings without a solicitor. These can all be found on the Court Service website, which also has online forms and links to the court rules.

Law on the Web

COM www.lawontheweb.co.uk

A very useful website with information on various legal topics, plus contact details, legal news, and a 'legal fun' page to cheer you up. Well worth a visit.

Compact Law

COM www.compactlaw.co.uk

This website has a considerable amount of information on most legal topics. You can also telephone a solicitor for further advice. At the time of publication, calls are charged at £1.50 per minute.

Generally, remember you can always get free advice from your local Citizens Advice Bureau, and your local Law Centre (if you are lucky enough to have one). See Part 2 for further details on sources of free advice generally.

Accidents, personal injury & medical negligence

If you or someone in your family has been involved in an accident, you may be entitled to claim for compensation. The majority of claims result from motor accidents. If the accident was not your fault, you will be able to claim compensation from the person who caused the accident, to cover any damage to your car and expenses arising from this, and also damages to compensate you for any personal injuries suffered by you as a result of the accident and any associated expenses. Personal injury claims can also arise out of accidents at work or an occupational disease, 'tripping' accidents where the local authority can be found liable for failing to maintain the highway properly, or you may be injured in holidays or travel abroad, or by a product you have purchased.

All these type of claims can be quite complex and it is best to obtain legal advice before doing anything, even if your claim is a very simple one. You should also keep an accurate record of all your expenses, keeping any estimates and receipts. If you are injured, you will need a medical report so go and see your doctor even if your injuries are slight, as this will also prove the fact that you were injured. It may be useful to keep a diary describing how the accident and injuries have affected your life. This will also prompt you to claim for your expenses properly, for example, travelling expenses to hospital.

If your claim arises from an accident you should obtain details of any witnesses, such as their names and addresses or car registration numbers, as you may need their evidence to prove that the accident was not your fault.

Some medical claims are not against the person who caused the injury but against your doctor or hospital for failing to treat you properly. These are called medical negligence claims. Medical negligence claims are invariably extremely complex and should not be attempted without legal assistance.

Getting advice

Although you may be able to get some free advice from your CAB, it is probably best to go straight to a solicitor. You may be contacted by unqualified 'claims advisors' offering assistance - if so, be careful, as they may be only interested in obtaining a percentage of your award. Do not sign anything without speaking to a solicitor first. It is not necessary to use one of the many referral agencies currently advertising no-win no-fee services; again these agencies will frequently wish to claim part of your award which will reduce your share. Also, they may allocate your case to a solicitor in a different town, or a long way away from you, who will be difficult for you to visit. If you do wish to use one of these agencies, be sure not to sign any payment forms for the insurance premium before you know who the solicitors will be and where they are located. Make sure you understand all the forms that you sign, and don't allow yourself to be rushed into anything.

As Legal Aid is no longer available for this type of claim, you will probably wish to have your claim dealt with on a no-win no-fee/conditional fee basis. Most solicitors offering these will say so in their Yellow Pages advertisement and therefore your local Yellow Pages is a good place to start looking. Accident Line is a scheme endorsed by the Law Society which will refer you to a specialist solicitor, who will give you an initial free interview. Unlike some other agencies, you will not have to pay any referral fee. All Accident Line solicitors are members of the Personal Injury Panel. There is also an Association of Personal Injury Lawyers ('APIL') who will able to advise you and refer you to specialist solicitors in your area. If your claim is a medical negligence claim, you should look for a solicitor who is experienced in this type of work as it is highly specialised. Try to use someone who is on the Law Society Clinical Negligence Panel or who is recommended by Action for Victims of Medical Accidents, a registered charity which has a free advisory service for victims of medical negligence.

Paying for advice

Most solicitors will give, at least, an initial free interview. Unfortunately, Legal Aid is no longer available for personal injury claims. However, most solicitors will be able to offer a no-win no-fee/conditional fee agreement. There are also many insurance firms that offer insurance policies to cover legal costs and expenses; your solicitor will normally be able to provide you with details. You may also be able to obtain free legal advice and assistance from your Trade Union, and some household or other insurance policies will include legal expenses insurance which could cover your claim. For example, travel insurance may cover claims regarding accidents abroad. Legal Aid is still available for medical negligence claims.

There are **Legal Services Commission booklets** on medical accidents and no-win, no-fee actions. For information on how to obtain these leaflets, see the section on the Legal Services Commission in Part 2.

Contacts:

Accident Line

COM www.accidentlinedirect.co.uk

This is the only referral scheme for personal injury claims backed by the Law Society. There is no referral fee. All solicitors in the scheme are members of the Personal Injury Panel.

Tel: 0800 192 939 (freephone)

Association of Personal Injury Lawyers

SOC www.apilonline.com

This association consists of solicitors and barrister who specialise in this work and is dedicated to improving the service given to victims of accidents and clinical negligence. The site gives some basic information and will give you a list of APIL members in your area. There is a link on the first page for people who are not APIL members.

33 Pilcher Gate
Nottingham NG1 1QE
Tel: 0115 958 0585
Email: mail@apil.com

Action for Victims of Medical Accidents

NFP www.avma.org.uk

A registered charity to assist persons who have suffered injury or harm as a result of inappropriate medical care, poor treatment or misdiagnosis/failure to diagnose. They can give free practical help and advice, for example, with the NHS complaints procedure, and if appropriate refer you to a suitable solicitor.

44 High Street
Croydon CR0 1YB
Tel: 020 8686 8333
Email - there is an online form on the website.

The Motor Accident Solicitors Society (MASS)

SOC www.mass.org.uk/homepage.htm

This is an association of solicitors' firms with experience and expertise in handling motor accident claims. They can refer you to a local solicitor who will give you an initial free consultation.

54 Baldwin Street
Bristol BS1 1QW
Tel: 0117 929 2560
Fax: 0117 904 7220
Email: office@mass.org.uk

These are some of the best contacts for you. However, there are many other internet sites that produce useful information about accident claims, a selection of which are set out below. You are also recommended to visit the section on Accidents and Injuries on Delia Venables' website, which will have a more complete and up to date listing.

Accident Compensation

COM www.accidentcompensation.com & www.medical-accidents.co.uk

Both these sites give information about compensation claims and can help you find a solicitor in your area. They do not make a charge for this.

Headway

NFP www.headway.org.uk

The National Head Injuries Association - a registered charity created to promote understanding of all aspects of head injury and to provide information, support and services to people with head injury, their family and carers.

Leigh Day & Co

COM www.leighday.co.uk

A solicitors' website with a lot of information about accident, personal injury, and medical negligence claims.

Medical Claims

COM www.medicalclaims.co.uk

This site has a lot of helpful information for patients who have suffered from poor medical care and can help you find a solicitor.

Can I Claim?

COM www.caniclaim.com

Another site with useful information and can also refer you to a solicitor. It is a free service.

In the following article, solicitor David Marshall discusses recent legislation regarding solicitors' fees in personal injury and accident claims.

'No-win no-fee' agreements

Many people believe that lawyers should share the risk of court cases with their clients rather than be paid their fees whatever the outcome. But public policy in England and Wales has long frowned on the ('American') idea that lawyers should be paid by their results in court cases. Backing a case in exchange for a 'share of the spoils', if it was won, was actually a criminal offence until 1967 and such agreements remained 'unenforceable' until 1995.

Conditional fee agreements ('CFAs')

In 1995, lawyers were allowed for the first time to take personal injury cases (extended in 1998 to all court cases, other than family and crime) under conditional fee agreements.

- A CFA is a type of 'contingency fee' arrangement. It provides that the lawyer is paid nothing (or, occasionally, a reduced fee) if the case is lost.

- It differs from an 'American-style' contingency fee in that if the case is won, the lawyer is not entitled to a cut of the money awarded, but instead gets a percentage increase on his normal hourly rate for the number of hours he has spent on the case (the 'success fee').

- The success fee cannot exceed 100 per cent (i.e. up to double his normal fee).

- The success fee can include:

  - a 'risk' element (the lawyer is running the risk of not being paid if the case is lost) and

  - a 'subsidy' element (the lawyer is not receiving payments on account of costs during the case, which he would normally receive from a private client or under the Community Legal Service (formerly Legal Aid).

- Solicitors can enter into a similar arrangement with specialist barristers on a client's behalf in appropriate cases.

It should be mentioned here that for claims to the Employment Tribunal, some solicitors will charge on an American-style percentage basis, which they are allowed to do at present, as claims to the Employment Tribunal are not classified as 'litigation'. Most CFAs are currently used for personal injury and accident claims.

Insurance

- 'After the event' policies: under English law, generally, the loser of a case is obliged to pay the winner his costs, so even though he has to pay his own lawyer nothing, a losing client instructing a lawyer under a CFA will need to take out an 'after the event' (ATE) legal expenses insurance policy to cover against this risk. (The ATE policy taken in conjunction with a CFA does not, of course, pay the client's own lawyer anything towards his lost fees if the case is lost.)

- 'Both sides costs' policies: CFAs and their accompanying ATE insurance should be distinguished from 'both sides costs' (BSC) insurance policies offered by certain insurance and 'claims management' companies. Both ATEs and BSCs tend to be described as 'no-win no-fee', but clients should be careful to ensure they know which they have signed up to. Although both schemes should lead to no cost if you lose (except sometimes payment of the ATE premium), there can be significant differences if you win.

- Some insurance companies also ask clients to enter into loan agreements to cover the cost of the ATE or BSC premiums, at significant interest rates - always think carefully before entering into any such loan and ask about the APR.

Recent legislation

On 1 April 2000, the Government made a significant change to the law relating to CFAs. Until that time, a winning client instructing a solicitor under a CFA would have to pay the success fee and the ATE premium himself, effectively out of any compensation he received when he won the case. However, because the Government removed personal injury cases from Legal Aid on the same date, they substantially improved the position of clients using CFAs.

For CFAs taken out after 1 April 2000, the 'risk element' of the success fee and the ATE insurance premium form part of the costs of the claim payable by the loser on top of any compensation. Unless the court specifically orders it, the lawyer is not allowed to charge to his client any part of the risk element that is not ordered to be paid by the loser. However, the subsidy element of the success fee (if any) is still down to the client.

Callery v. Gray

Unfortunately, after April 2000, a substantial log-jam of CFA cases arose in the courts. This was created because insurance companies representing defendants who had lost cases, being asked to pay the risk elements of success fees and the ATE premiums, raised a number of technical legal arguments about the scope of government reforms. These arguments had to be decided by the Court of Appeal in a case called Callery v Gray.

Judgment was given in July 2001. The defendant insurance companies' technical arguments were rejected and the Court of Appeal ordered that they had to pay the risk element of reasonable success fees (20 per cent was allowed for moderate and straightforward road traffic accidents).

The Court also said that the loser had to pay reasonable ATE premiums, but it was less clear about how much is considered reasonable. There will have to be more court cases over subsequent months and years to decide this. This is particularly important because (unlike the risk element in success fees) clients are usually obliged to pay the ATE or BSC premium in full if they win, even if they can only recover part of it from their opponent.

So with a CFA linked to a reasonable ATE policy, the lawyers' costs and success fee and the ATE premium should all be recoverable from the loser, leaving the client with his compensation largely intact.

Looking at the agreement CFA in more detail - three examples

These examples will give you an idea of how the various rules and regulations which affect CFAs could work out in practice. In this hypothetical case, an award is made of £5,000, plus a costs award of £1,750 (although the costs actually incurred in fact came to £2,000), plus 'disbursements' (mainly court fees and medical reports) of £500.

In the first two examples, there was an ATE insurance premium of £350, in the third example there was a BSC premium of £1,250. This was paid by a consumer credit loan, which by the time the case had ended, had accrued interest of £350.

Example 1

Note that:

- Solicitors are usually entitled to charge a small extra sum to their client over and above the sum recovered from the loser.

- Solicitors are also entitled to charge the subsidy element of the success fee.

- The solicitor is required to specify in the CFA his hourly rates, the success fee (split between risk and subsidy elements) and the reasons for the success fee.

So:

- Ask whether the solicitor's hourly rate is the same as he expects to recover from the other side, so that you will not be landed with a bill for a shortfall in rates.

- If you win and a subsidy element is charged, ask how this is calculated. If this relates partly to disbursements to be paid on your behalf by the solicitor and you have sufficient funds to meet them yourself, considering doing so to reduce the cost.

- Also check the price of the ATE premium and ask whether the solicitor expects to recover its cost in full from the loser if you win.

Example:

Item	Expenses	Receipts	Balances
Compensation	0	5,000	5,000
Basic costs	2,000	1,750	-250
Success fee ('risk')	400	400	0
Success fee ('subsidy')	200	0	-200
Disbursements	500	500	0
ATE premium	350	350	0
Totals	*3,450*	*8,000*	*4,550*

Example 2

Many solicitors, as a matter of course, charge nothing for the subsidy element of the success fee (accepting this cost themselves as a business expense) and will voluntarily waive any basic costs not recovered from the loser.

The Indemnity Principle: So far as waiving costs not recovered is concerned, solicitors may be reluctant to agree formally to this in advance because of an obscure technical rule called the 'indemnity principle'. In brief, this means that if a solicitor agrees in advance to accept only what he can recover in costs from the other side, he may be entitled to receive no costs at all.

This rule is also one of the main reasons why the documents for CFAs are so ludicrously complex. This rule is currently subject to review. As soon as it is abolished, all CFAs can become simpler and more transparent.

In the meantime, if a reputable solicitors' firm says that it will charge nothing for the 'subsidy element' of the success fee and that it is their usual practice to waive irrecoverable basic costs, you can probably believe them. This provides a good deal to the consumer as it is 'no-win, no-cost' and 'win, no-cost'.

Example:

Item	Expenses	Receipts	Balances
Compensation	0	5,000	5,000
Basic costs	1,750	1,750	0
Success fee ('risk')	400	400	0
Success fee ('subsidy')	0	0	0
Disbursements	500	500	0
ATE premium	350	350	0
Totals	*3,000*	*8,000*	*5,000*

Example 3

This shows the possible scenario of a 'BSC' or ATE policy where the Court refuses to allow the full premium to be paid back to the winning client.

At the time of writing no such case is known to have been so decided by a Court, but an indication of this possibility was given by the Court of Appeal in Callery v Gray. Before agreeing to any such arrangement, the question about possible irrecoverability of the premium should be put to the solicitor and/or any claims manager.

Example:

Item	Liabilities	Receipts	Balances
Compensation	0	5,000	5,000
Basic costs	1,750	1,750	0
Success fee ('risk')	0	0	0
Success fee ('subsidy')	0	0	0
Disbursements	500	500	0
BSC premium (say)	1,250	350	-900
Interest on premium loan (say)	350	0	-350
Totals	*3,000*	*8,000*	*3,750*

The three examples show how three different arrangements, probably all marketed as 'no-win, no-fee', would indeed all leave the client with no liability for costs if the case were lost, but with very different net recoveries for the client if the case were won.

How much control does the insurer have?

Another issue to raise with your lawyer is the degree of control any ATE insurer may have over the conduct of the case, especially if a settlement offer is made. It is also worth asking what happens if there is a Part 36 payment (a formal offer to settle the case, which, if refused, puts the client at risk of paying all the costs afterwards) into court in attempted settlement.

Arguably, giving the lawyer - or ATE or BSC - insurer a financial interest in the outcome might create possible conflicts of interest (e.g. when advising whether or not to accept a settlement offer, acceptance of which would trigger payment of the lawyer's fees under a CFA or relieve the ATE or BSC insurer of any further risk of liability). These conflicts are worse under some CFA arrangements than others. Some ATE or BSC insurers exercise more influence than others. Clearly, identifying whether there might be a problem is easier at the outset than at the time it happens.

Finding a lawyer

Market forces and consumer awareness do not yet properly operate in the relatively new market of CFA cases. The technicalities are complex and are relatively untested in the courts. Extreme care should be taken to choose a legal representative who can represent you competently, to win the case, and get proper compensation at little or no cost to you. Even in the most straightforward cases, the differences in net recovery for the client could be substantial.

- The Law Society maintains a list of members of their Personal Injury Panel.

- The Association of Personal Injury Lawyers (APIL) can put you in touch with specialist firms that have a Fellow of the College of Personal Injury Law.

- Best of all is probably a reliable personal recommendation.

Note: Some of the companies marketing for this work are consortia of specialist solicitors' firms. Others are claims managers or insurance providers. Be sure you know whom you are dealing with and that you are happy with your choice.

Obviously, the use of CFAs means that lawyers are only going to take on a case if they are reasonably sure that they are going to win. If they think:

- that you are unlikely to prove that the accident was someone else's fault; or

- that your injuries were not caused by the accident; or

- that the compensation is below the Small Claims limit (currently £1,000 for injury cases);

then they won't take on your case.

However, if you do have a reasonably good case, it should not be difficult to find a good lawyer willing to help you.

Your responsibilities

Under a CFA, you will have responsibilities to pursue the claim and to help the lawyer; do so by cooperating, attending medical appointments and so on. You must also check whether you have legal expenses insurance under any personal insurance policy, which would cover your costs, taken out by you 'before the event'. If you do, and provided that it is appropriate cover, you will probably find it difficult to justify signing a CFA, taking out an ATE policy and claiming the cost back from the loser.

In conclusion

Government reforms should mean that if you have got a reasonably good case, then not only should you be able to get a 'no-win no-fee' deal, but also, if you shop around, you should be able to secure a 'win, no-cost' arrangement, too.

David Marshall

David Marshall is a partner with London firm, Anthony Gold, Solicitors. He is Treasurer of APIL. He is a Fellow of the College of Personal Injury Law, a Fellow of the Society for Advanced Legal Studies and a Member of the Law Society's Personal Injury Panel. He has written and lectured extensively on the subject of CFAs and other personal injury matters.

Business matters: company & commercial

This book is aimed principally at consumers rather than the business community and therefore this section is a small one. However, the Law Society's 'Lawyers for your Business' scheme must be mentioned.

Lawyers for your Business

Lawyers for your Business is administered by the Law Society and backed by Business in the Community, the Federation of Small Businesses, and the Forum of Private Business. Under this scheme participating lawyers will give a free diagnostic interview. You can find solicitors participating in this scheme in your local Yellow Pages or by ringing the Law Society on 020 7405 9075. They will send you a list plus a voucher for the free advice session.

You can also obtain useful free guides by calling 01689 850 227.

You can find out more about this scheme from the Law Society's website. Go first to www.solicitors-online.com and follow the link for business help.

The Business debtline
Tel: 0800 197 6026
For help and advice in dealing with business debts.

Companies House
GOV   www.companieshouse.gov.uk

This is where all company records are kept. You can do a free online search to find out basic information about any registered company, such as its registered office address. You can also search the database of disqualified company directors. There is a considerable amount of information online such as guidance booklets and FAQs. You can fill in most company forms online to print off and post for filing and you can find out information about filing documents electronically. There is also a full list of all Companies House prices. If you have any involvement with limited companies, this is a good site to visit.

There are offices in London, Cardiff, Birmingham, Manchester, Leeds, Glasgow and Birmingham. You can make email enquiries using an online form.

Charities

If you are setting up or running a charity, then you need to be sure that you are doing things properly and that you are taking advantage of all the tax and other concessions available to charities. The first step is to register with the Charity Commission, whose details are given below. They will be able to provide you with all the information you will need for this, and have many other leaflets of assistance in running charities and fund-raising.

If you need more detailed advice, there are solicitors who specialise in charity law. It is probably best to find these by personal recommendation (e.g. from the CAB) or you can use the Solicitors Online website.

The Charity Commission

GOV www.charity-commission.gov.uk

This is the official site of the Charity Commission and contains much useful information and guidance for those running charities. The site contains all the Commission's leaflets and a list of publications, many of which you can download in PDF format. You can also search the register of charities. There are three offices, in London, Liverpool and Taunton.

London Office
Harmsworth House
13-15 Bouverie Street
London EC4Y 8DP
Tel: 0870 333 0123
Fax: 020 7674 2300
Central Register open between 9am and 5pm

Liverpool Office
20 Kings Parade
Queens Dock
Liverpool L3 4DQ
Tel: 0870 333 0123
Fax: 0151 703 1555
Central Register open between 9am and 4.30pm

Taunton Office
Woodfield House
Tangier, Taunton
Somerset TA1 4BL
Tel: 0870 333 0123
Fax: 01823 345 003
Central Register open between 9.30am and 4pm

There are also a number of helplines:

All general enquiries: 0870 333 0123

Annual return helpline: 0151 703 1515
Registration helpline, help for existing charities and concerns about fundraising: 0870 333 0123
The number for hearing and speech impaired callers using a minicom is: 0870 333 0125

Charities Aid Foundation

NFP www.cafonline.org

A non-government organisation that helps charities with fundraising and gives support and information. Also of interest to those who wish to donate to charity. A helpful website.

Main Office
Kings Hill
West Malling
Kent ME19 4TA
Tel: 01732 520 000
Fax: 01732 520 001
Email: info@caf.charitynet.org

Children

This section is for children themselves, not about them. If you are under 18 and need help, for example, if you are being abused or bullied, then the contacts in this section may help you. Some of them are specifically for children in care; the others are for all children.

All children have their fears and their worries. Very few feel able to talk about them. However, you should try to speak to someone, particularly if your problems involve any kind of abuse. Breaking the silence will only help you. Somehow the very fact of speaking something out loud to another person changes it; you find you have a new view of your problem and may be able to find solutions you could not think of when just thinking to yourself. Strange, but true.

Often the best person to talk to is a member of your family. If this is not possible, then talk to a sympathetic teacher at school. They are there to help you. However, if your problem is a serious one, they will be under an obligation to do something about it, and this may involve telling your parents. You may feel that you do not want this at present.

If you feel unable to discuss your problem with anyone you know, try speaking to one of the services below. They are confidential and free, and you do not have to identify yourself if you do not want to.

ChildLine

Freephone: 0800 1111

ChildLine is a free national 24-hour telephone helpline for any child in trouble or danger. It is a confidential counselling service that offers information and help to children and young people.

ChildLine also runs a separate helpline for children in care on 0800 884 444, open daily between 6pm and 10pm.

Kidscape

NFP www.kidscape.org.uk

A national charity committed to keeping children safe from harm or abuse. The website has a good section on bullying and they have a bullying counsellor available between 10am and 4pm weekdays.

Bullying Counsellor - Tel: 020 7730 3300

2 Grosvenor Gardens
London SW1W 0DH
Tel: 020 7730 3300
Fax: 020 7730 7081
Email: contact@kidscape.org.uk

NSPCC (National Society for the Protection of Cruelty to Children)

NFP www.nspcc.org.uk

The website has information about the work of the NSPCC. You can also find out NSPCC publications and how to make donations.

NSPCC Children Protection Helpline: 0800 800 500
This is a free national 24-hour service that provides counselling, information and advice to anyone, including children, concerned about a child at risk.

The Samaritans

NFP www.samaritans.org.uk

The Samaritans is a registered charity based in the UK and Republic of Ireland that provides confidential emotional non-judgmental support to any person (including any child) who needs to talk to someone, particularly if you are suicidal or despairing. They are open 24 hours a day every day. You can telephone, visit or email them. Ring or visit their website to find your local branch.

Tel: 0845 790 9090 (UK) or 1850 60 9090 (Republic of Ireland)
Email: jo@samaritans.org

Who Cares Trust

Telephone linkline: 0500 564 570

This freecall telephone linkline service provides support and information to children and young people in care. It is open Mondays, Wednesdays and Thursdays between 3pm and 6.30pm.

Carelaw

NFP www.nchafc.org.uk/carelaw

This is a site created for children in care, with information that is updated every six months. It is very comprehensive.

National Youth Advocacy Service

This has an advocacy service for children in care. Any young person looked after by a Local Authority may ring the:

Free Phoneline on 0800 616 101. Lines are open between 3.30pm and 9.30pm every weekday and between 2pm and 8pm on Saturdays and Sundays.

1 Downham Road South
Heswall, Wirral
Merseyside L60 5RG
Tel: 0151 342 7852
Fax: 0151 342 3174

Young Minds

NFP www.youngminds.org.uk

This is a charity that aims to help young people who are feeling troubled or distressed. When viewing the website, follow the link from the shoes picture.

102-108 Clerkenwell Road
London EC1M 5SA
Tel: 020 7336 8445
Fax: 020 7336 8446
Email: enquiries@youngminds.org.uk

Youthnet

NFP www.youthnet.org.uk/health.html

This website has lots of useful information on different topics of interest to young people. You can also use it to find local organisations that can help you.

Co-habitees - see 'Family' section.

Consumer problems

There are many rights that consumers have which are enshrined in statute. Many of these are regulated by Trading Standards (see p88). However, for general information, a few of the most important are as follows:

- **Consumer Credit Act 1974:** This Act provides for organisations offering credit to be regulated, and regulates the granting of credit generally. Two provisions of the Act are of particular importance to consumers. The first of these is section 75 which provides that a creditor will (normally) be jointly and severally liable with a supplier for any misrepresentation or breach of contract. Thus, if you buy a car with your Visa card you can also claim against the bank if the car is faulty and the garage goes out of business. The second provision is the cooling-off period of seven days that consumers normally have under contracts that are signed away from the traders' place of business. The Consumer Credit Act is a major piece of protective legislation for the consumer; however, it is a very complex and difficult Act in many ways. Legal advice should therefore be sought before enforcing any of its provisions. Your local Trading Standards Office is a good place to go for free initial advice.

- **The Unfair Contract Terms Act 1977:** This makes illegal a number of contract term types in contracts with consumers, such as excluding liability for death or personal injury where the business has been negligent, preventing unreasonable restrictions on liability resulting from breach of contract, preventing business from claiming that they can perform under the contract in a way that is substantially different from what could be reasonably expected or do nothing at all, and preventing guarantees from being used to restrict liability in negligence for defective goods

- **Sale of Goods Act 1979:** This Act affects sales of goods in particular to consumers, for example, goods sold must be fit for the purpose for which they are sold and be of satisfactory quality. Often sellers imply to customers that the only protection they have is under their own guarantee - this is not the case; all sales of goods to consumers will have the protection of the Sale of Goods Act, and this protection can last up to six years after the sale.

- **Supply of Goods and Services Act 1982:** This is a similar act that covers services to consumers rather than sale of goods. Subject to any agreed contract terms, the service performed must be to a reasonable standard and be done within a reasonable time for a reasonable price.

- **The Unfair Terms in Consumer Contracts Regulations 1999:** This provides that any terms in standard consumer contracts that are 'unfair', i.e. which cause a significant imbalance in the parties' rights and obligations to the detriment to the consumer, are void. Terms must be in 'plain English'. The regulations do not apply to 'core terms' (apart from the requirement to be in plain English which covers all terms). 'Core terms' are terms which say what the subject matter of the contract is and give the price. Terms, which are deemed 'unfair' under the regulations, cannot be enforced at law. The Office of Fair Trading have set up an Unfair Contract Terms Unit which is considering standard terms with a view to giving guidance on standard contract types. Their contact details appear below.

- **Distance Selling Regulations:** These regulations protect consumers when purchasing items and services at a distance, e.g. by mail order, telephone or on the internet. For example, you are normally entitled to a cancellation period of at least seven days, the period starting from the time you were informed of your rights under the regulations or 30 days, whichever is the shorter. (See also the section on Internet law, below).

There are of course many other statutes that address consumer issues. Most of these are summarised online on the Trading Standards Net website.

Many consumers are denied their rights by businesses, as popular programmes, such as BBC's 'Watchdog', show. As the value of consumer claims are often not more than a few hundred pounds, it is usually best not to pay a solicitor for advice, as solicitors' charges will soon exceed the value of the claim. Generally, sufficient advice can be obtained for free, for example, from the CAB or Trading Standards. However, if it is necessary to take the trader to court (usually the Small Claims Court), then it may be helpful just to talk the case over with a solicitor to ensure that you are going about things in the right way. Many solicitors will offer a free or fixed price initial interview for this type of thing. You can also obtain helpful leaflets about bringing proceedings from your local County Court or from the court service website. Remember that if you are on benefit or a low income you may not have to pay court fees. For further information, ask the court office.

The Unfair Contract Terms Unit

Office of Fair Trading
Room 505 Field House
15-25 Breams Buildings
London EC4A 1PR
Tel: 020 7211 8446
Fax: 020 7211 8404

Trading Standards

www.tradingstandards.gov.uk

Trading Standards offices are departments of Local Authorities, and their statutory function is to regulate and enforce a vast body of legislation whose principal function is the protection of the public. A full list of this legislation can be found on the main Trading Standards website.

Trading Standards departments vary from Local Authority to Local Authority. However, all of them have developed a vast bank of knowledge on consumer topics and they will be very happy to help and advise the general public on matters that fall within their remit. Many will have a dedicated telephone line for telephone advice. Space does not permit printing these in full here, but telephone numbers can be found from your telephone directory or Yellow Pages. Many Trading Standards offices also have a consumer education programme and will, for example, give talks at local schools.

Consumers: Trading Standards' main duty is to investigate and, if necessary, prosecute under their statutory powers. However, they will, if possible, try to assist consumers to obtain compensation in suitable cases, either by requesting a compensation order in legal proceedings against traders or through discussions with them. This is not something consumers can demand of their Trading Standards office as of right. However, for a consumer problem, which does not involve more than a few hundred pounds, consumers are probably better advised to consult their local Trading Standards office first, rather than consult a solicitor (whose fees could soon equal, if not exceed, the value of the goods in question).

Businesses: Also, Trading Standards are always happy to give advice and assistance to businesses. Generally, they would much prefer to assist a business to stay within the law than to bring a prosecution. Businesses who are worried about the standards they have to comply with should always consult their local Trading Standards office.

Publications: There are many helpful leaflets and information booklets available from Trading Standards offices giving advice on many topics. Many of these can also be downloaded from the Trading Standards website.

Main areas of operation: Very generally, these are as follows:

- the motor industry - e.g. substandard vehicles, 'clocking' of cars, general service levels;
- the tourist industry - e.g. poor standards, misdescriptions of holidays, timeshare properties;

- home improvements - e.g. workmanship of builders and craftsmen;
- faulty and counterfeit goods - e.g. consumer goods such as electrical goods, toys, computers, etc.;
- consumer credit - e.g. the purchase of goods and services on credit;
- food - e.g. labelling and food constitution (the Environmental Health Departments of Local Authorities will deal with hygiene matters and foreign bodies in food);
- livestock on farms - e.g. licensing, transportation, animal feedstuffs;
- product safety - e.g. unsafe toys and electrical goods, routine sampling of standard goods and testing to ensure safety.

You can find details of your local Trading Standards office from your Local Authority; details can also be found on the Trading Standards Net website below.

The Office of Fair Trading

GOV www.oft.gov.uk

The OFT is less accessible than Trading Standards offices and tends to do more general work, setting standards and preparing reports. The website has a good selection of information pages and reports and is well worth looking at. There is, for example, a useful 'Consumer alert' series that gives information about current scams consumers need to be wary of, or new rights consumers have acquired.

OFT public enquiry number: 0845 722 4499
This is a number which you can ring for general advice. However, the OFT is unable to help on individual cases. You can also email the OFT.
Email: enquiries@oft.gov.uk

The Consumer Gateway

GOV www.consumer.gov.uk

This is a government service with useful information on a variety of topics and contact details where you can find out more.

The Consumers Association/Which?

NFP www.which.net

This organisation campaigns on behalf of consumers and produces a magazine (only available on subscription) giving reports on consumer testing and problems encountered by consumers. The website has details of their product testing reports together with other useful information and details of 'Which?' publications. There are also online forums.

Which? also offers a Which? Legal Service which, on payment of an annual subscription, will provide legal advice by telephone. Further written advice can be obtained for a fixed fee. Contact the customer service team, or follow the legal link on the website for details.

Which?
Castlemead
Gascoyne Way
Hertford SG14 1YB

The Which Customer Service Team: 0645 830 240 between 9am and 9pm Monday to Friday, between 9am and 3pm on Saturdays.
Fax: 020 7770 7485
Email at support@which.net

Trading Standards Net

NFP www.tradingstandards.net

This useful website has much helpful information for consumers, including details of consumer legislation, self-help letters, articles on current issues and details of latest product recalls. There is also advice on a wide variety of topics from airbag cartridges to video recordings, and a very good links page.

How to Complain

COM www.howtocomplain.com

A very useful site which guides you through the process of making a complaint. There is help and information on a very wide variety of situations and the procedure of making a complaint is explained carefully.

Consumer Solicitors

COM   www.consumer-solicitors.co.uk

This is a commercial site with much useful information on a wide variety of consumer topics.

Crime

If you are a victim

There are two sides to every crime - the victim and the offender. All too often, most of the attention is given to the offender rather than to the victim. This is now beginning to change, but there is no doubt that being the victim of any crime can be a traumatic experience. However, there is an organisation, Victim Support, which can give assistance.

Victim Support

NFP   www.victimsupport.com

Victim Support is the national charity for people affected by crime. It is a completely independent organisation, offering a free and confidential service, irrespective of whether or not a crime has been reported. The website gives full details of the service given, and also details of how you can help. There is a victim support line, which can help you, whether the crime is recent or past, and whether or not you want to report the crime. It can provide information, practical help or support.

PO Box 11431
London SW9 6ZH
Victim Supportline: 0845 303 0900 between 9am and 9pm Mondays to Fridays; 9am and 7pm weekends; 9am and 5pm bank holidays. All calls are confidential and charged at local rates.
Email: supportline@victimsupport.org.uk

If you are accused of a crime

If you are accused of a crime, whether or not you are guilty, you should seek legal advice as soon as possible. The best person to seek advice from is a solicitor who is part of the Criminal Defence Service.

The Criminal Defence Service

OFF www.legalservices.gov.uk/cds/index.htm

There have been great changes recently in the delivery of the Legal Aid service available for those accused of crime. As discussed in the section on Legal Aid and the Community Legal Service in Part 2, in April 2000 the Legal Aid Board became the Legal Services Commission and this now administers the new Criminal Defence Service. Solicitors' firms will now only carry out criminal defence work if they have a contract with the Legal Services Commission, and will have to meet the LSC's stringent quality standards. This means that there are now fewer firms who will do this work, and your previous solicitor may no longer be offering a criminal advocacy service. The CDS is also piloting a system where they directly employ a number of criminal defence lawyers, known as public defenders, who will do the same defence work as the solicitors' firms.

To find a solicitors' firm or public defender in your area, you can ring the CLS Call Centre on 0845 608 1122; Minicom 0845 609 6677 (all calls are charged at local rates) or consult the Just Ask website - www.justask.org.uk.

The duty solicitor service

At the police station: If the police question you about an offence, whether or not you have been arrested, you have a right to free legal advice from a contracted solicitor. There is no means test for this advice. You should ask the police to contact the duty solicitor or your own solicitor, if you have one.

At court: If you have to go to the magistrate's court on a criminal case and do not have your own solicitor, there will usually be a duty solicitor available either at the court or on call to give you free advice and representation on your first appearance. Again, there is no means test. Ask the court staff for the duty solicitor. However, it is best, if possible, to get advice before you go to court.

There are **Legal Services Commission booklets** on the criminal defence service, criminal defence services at the police station and in court, and dealing with the police. To find out how to obtain these booklets, see the section on the Legal Services Commission in Part 2.

The Police

OFF www.police.uk

The police are our guardians and exist to protect us from crime and to guarantee our civil liberties. However, all too often they are viewed, justly or unjustly, as quite the reverse of this. Whatever your views on the police, however, they are the first organisation that should be contacted if a crime has been committed (evidence of reporting a crime to the police will also often be required by your insurers if you need to claim on your insurance policy). Your local police station can be found in the telephone directory, or in an emergency, they can be contacted via the emergency telephone line 999.

Information about your local police force, plus non-geographic services and related organisations can be found on the website.

As well as their primary function of investigating crime, the police will also advise on related issues such as home security, and will generally give talks, for example, in schools, on police work.

Crimestoppers

This is a national organisation, well known for their television broadcasts, which the public can contact anonymously to report a crime.

Freephone: 0800 555 111

The Police Complaints Authority

OFF www.pca.gov.uk

The independent PCA supervises investigations into complaints against police officers. As a member of the public, you can make a complaint about the conduct of a police officer towards yourself if you think you have good reason, or you can complain on someone else's behalf if you have their written authorisation. Further details are available on the website

10 Great George Street
London SW1P 3AE
General enquiries, tel: 020 7273 6450
Email: info@pca.gov.uk

Police Stop

NFP www.policestop.org.uk

This interesting and comprehensive site provides links to all UK Police and Emergency Services links, and associated UK Government links. There are separate sections for Scottish and Northern Ireland sources. There are also international links relating to crime, police and detection, and numerous pictures.

Debt advice

See also 'Finance, banks & consumer credit problems' section.

If you have financial problems, it is important to take action and get the problem under control sooner rather than later. There are many organisations that can offer advice and help. However, it is best to seek help from a well-known and reputable organisation such as the Citizens Advice Bureau, rather than by answering an advertisement in the paper. Some commercial debt advice organisations will try to get you to take out a new loan (upon which they will get commission) to pay off all your debts. However, this is not normally recommended, as it will generally end up being more expensive for you in the long run. Others will make substantial charges for their work, which again is undesirable.

As well as the CAB, you may find that there are local 'not for profit' debt advice agencies in your town, which are usually very good. Contact your local authority for details.

There is a **Legal Services Commission booklet** on dealing with debt. For information on how to obtain these leaflets, see the section on the Legal Services Commission in Part 2.

If your financial affairs are in such a state that you feel that bankruptcy is the only option, then take advice before doing anything. Visit the Insolvency Service website and consider taking advice from an Insolvency Practitioner ('IP'). These are specialists who have passed a stiff set of examinations in insolvency law and are licensed by the Government. Insolvency Practitioners generally work either for accountants or for solicitors' firms. If you consult an IP in a solicitors' firm that is part of the

Community Legal Service, you may be able to get free advice. However, most of the accountancy based IPs also offer free advice sessions. Make sure though that you are given full details of all their charges before you authorise them to act for you.

The Insolvency Service

GOV
REC

www.insolvency.gov.uk

This is the Government department that deals with bankruptcies and company windings up. It is an extremely informative site and there are leaflets you can read and download on various aspects of insolvency, such as 'A Guide to Bankruptcy' and 'What will happen to my home?' There is also advice on how to petition for bankruptcy and you can download the forms from the site. Other advice includes information on insolvency practitioners and how to find one local to you, and a hotline to report undischarged bankrupts and disqualified company directors who are disregarding the disqualification orders made against them.

There are numerous insolvency offices throughout the country, and therefore they are not all listed here. You can find your local office from the website or by calling the Central Public Enquiry Line.

Central Public Enquiry Line: 020 7291 6895 currently available between 9am and 5pm Monday to Friday.
Email: central.enquiryline@insolvency.gsi.gov.uk

The Consumer Debt Counselling Service

Freephone: 0800 138 1111
This is a service run by the Foundation for Credit Counselling, and gives counselling and other help to people in debt.

The National Debtline

Tel: 0845 950 0511
This service will give you advice and help for personal debts.

The Business Debtline

Freephone: 0800 197 6026
For advice and help in dealing with business debts.

Credit Action

www.creditaction.com

This is a Christian money education charity promoting self-help in personal money matters. There is some helpful online information and you can purchase their books. They also operate a debt management helpline.

Debt management helpline: 0800 591 084
6 Regent Terrace
Cambridge CB2 1AA
Tel/Fax: 01223 324 034
Email: credit.action@dial.pipex.com

Divorce - see 'Family' section.

Domestic violence - see 'Family' section.

Education

This area of law covers problems relating to a child's right to education, for example, with relation to the child's special needs, as well as problems with further education. The best place to go for initial advice is probably the CAB's 'advice guide' website. This is a specialised area of work and if you need a lawyer the best place to locate one is via the Just Ask website. Mediation is also sometimes available for problems in education - see further in the mediation section.

The Children's Legal Centre

www2.essex.ac.uk/clc

This organisation is concerned with law and policy affecting children and young people. There is a free information service for children and young people and anyone with concerns about them. There is also a legal education advocacy unit - this operates only within south east England but advice and mediation services can be offered to those outside this area.

University of Essex
Wivenhoe Park
Colchester
Essex CO4 3SQ
Advice line: 01206 873 820 (Opening Times: between 10am and
12.30pm and 2pm and 4.30pm Monday to Friday)
Education Legal Advocacy Unit, tel: 01206 873 966
Fax: 01206 874 026
Email: clc@essex.ac.uk

The Office for Standards in Education (Ofsted)

GOV www.ofsted.gov.uk

This is the official website of Ofsted, where you can find out about
their work and do a search for reports on your child's school. You
can also see a list of their publications and order them online.

Employment law

This is a very important and complex area of law. It is also an area where
the law has changed considerably over the past few years (as both a result
of new legislation and the development of case and European law), and
where changes are likely to continue into the foreseeable future. Because
it is such a rapidly changing area of law, there is considerable ignorance,
among both employers and employees, as to what their respective rights
and obligations currently are. The following are some areas where there are
often problems or uncertainty:

- **Contracts of employment** - many employers are still not providing
  their employees with contracts, even though it is an employee's
  statutory right to be provided with a written statement of the main
  terms of the contract after he has been in employment for two
  months.

- **Changes to the contract of employment** - often an employer will want
  to change an employee's terms of employment and this can cause
  problems.

- **Payment and deductions from wages** - employees often find that
  money is deducted, for example, in respect of till shortages from their
  wages without their consent.

- **Handling sickness and other absences** - there is frequently uncertainty among both employers and employees as to an employee's rights where he has had time off from work other than his holiday entitlement.

- **Unfair dismissals and redundancy** - again a complex area and one where both parties will often need advice.

- **Discrimination** - there is currently legislation in place to protect employees from discrimination on the grounds of their sex, race or disability, with recourse to the Employment Tribunal in cases where these rights are broken.

Time limit for claims to Employment Tribunal: Employees should note that if they intend to make a claim to the Employment Tribunal, this should normally be done within **three months** of the event complained of (usually the date of dismissal), otherwise the claim will fail. Advice should therefore be sought as soon as possible after the event, if there is any possibility of a claim being made. Save in very exceptional circumstances, (such as the employee being unable to make a claim due to serious illness) the tribunal will not allow any claim if it is submitted to the tribunal office after the three month period has expired.

There are a number of sources of free information and advice for employment law, the most important being ACAS. Many employees will also be able to take advice from their Trade Union. These are discussed in detail below, after which follow some other useful sources of advice and information.

There is a **Legal Services Commission booklet** on employment - your rights at work. For information on how to obtain these leaflets, see the section on the Legal Services Commission in Part 2.

Advisory, Conciliation and Arbitration Services (ACAS)

OFF www.acas.org.uk

This is an independent service that was set up in 1974. It is funded by the Department of Trade and Industry, but is independent and impartial. Its mission statement is to improve the performance and effectiveness of organisations by providing an independent and impartial service to prevent and resolve disputes and to build harmonious relationships at work. All information given to ACAS is held in confidence.

To pursue its mission, ACAS has four key areas of work:

1. **Individual conciliation:** When a claim is made to an employment tribunal, papers are also automatically sent to ACAS and an ACAS officer is allocated to the case, who will endeavour to promote a settlement of the case without the need of a tribunal hearing. This is an extremely helpful service and one which should be used whenever possible. Parties should not view participating in conciliation as 'giving in' or 'letting them get away with it'. Tribunals will expect parties to reach agreement if possible and parties who refuse reasonable offers of settlement may be penalised in costs. Of course, it is possible to reach agreement other than via the ACAS service. However, employers in particular are recommended to use the ACAS conciliation service, particularly if they do not have legal representation. The reason for this is that when a settlement is reached via ACAS, a form of agreement (called a COT3 form) prepared by the ACAS officer is signed by both parties which is legally binding upon them. A 'home-made' agreement will not be binding in the same way unless it has certain legal clauses incorporated into it and is signed by the employee's legal advisor as well as the employee.

2. **Collective conciliation:** This service, which conciliates in workplace disputes, is normally carried out as a result of being called in by Trades Unions or the employer. Typical situations where ACAS will be called in are where the employer does not consult Trades Unions when making large-scale redundancies or where there is industrial action. Both parties have to consent to the conciliation.

3. **Advisory mediation projects:** For this service ACAS will, through a serious of working parties, explore with both parties issues that cause problems in the workplace, and try to find solutions. Frequently, this service arises out of a workplace dispute where ACAS has been called in, when during the mediation process it become apparent that this service would help future employee-employer relations.

4. **Promoting good practice:** This area of work can be broken down into a number of different services, all coming under the umbrella of promoting good practice:

- *Public enquiry points* - All regional offices have manned telephone lines (between 9am and 5pm) to answer queries from the public. Both employees and employers can use the service. Only information, not advice, will be given. This is an extremely helpful service for everyone in the workplace. A list of all the regional telephone numbers appears below.

- *ACAS publications* - ACAS publish many useful guides, reports and leaflets. Some are free and others have a modest charge. Some of the ACAS guides and codes are accepted by tribunals as setting out the standards that will be expected of employers (such as the ACAS code of practice for disciplinary and grievance procedures). A list of publications can be obtained by ringing any of the ACAS telephone numbers or can be found online on the ACAS website

- *Small firms seminars/workshops* - These take place regularly around the country on a variety of topics. Details can be found by ringing the public enquiry points or from the ACAS website.

- *Talks* - Again these can be on a variety of topics. Details of local talks near you can be found by ringing the public enquiry points or from the ACAS website.

- *The ACAS website* - This provides details of the ACAS services as discussed above, and also gives some news and other items on employment matters. It is a useful site to find out about the services offered by ACAS but does not, as yet, contain much legal information.

ACAS Public Enquiry Points:

- Birmingham (0121) 456 5856
- Bristol (0117) 946 9500
- Cardiff (029) 2076 1126
- Fleet (01252) 811 868
- Glasgow (0141) 204 2677
- Leeds (0113) 243 1371
- Liverpool (0151) 427 8881
- London (020) 7396 5100
- Manchester (0161) 833 8585
- Newcastle upon Tyne (0191) 261 2191
- Nottingham (0115) 969 3355

ACAS Head Office
Brandon House
180 Borough High Street
London SE1 1LW

The Health & Safety Executive

GOV   www.hse.gov.uk

The HSE is a government service that deals primarily with issues concerning health and safety at work, although they also deal with other health and safety issues, such as domestic gas. Their main role is to ensure that risks to health and safety from work activities are properly controlled. The HSE primarily has an advisory role. However, it also enforces some Health and Safety legislation, and details of prosecutions can be found on the website.

If you have a problem about health and safety at work, you can contact the HSE for advice. You can use their advice line, contact your local office, or one of their information centres.

HSE Infoline: 0870 154 5500, open between 8.30am and 5pm
                        Monday to Friday.
Fax: 029 2085 9260
Email: hseinformationservices@natbrit.com

There is also a feedback form and full details of all the HSE offices on the website.

Trade Unions

For a general introduction on Trade Unions and the general services they offer see the section in Part 2.

The bulk of the services offered by Trade Unions to their members relate to problems in the workplace. If a sufficient number of workers in a firm are members of a particular union, then by law that Trade Union must be 'recognised' by the employer. This means that the Union must be consulted on all matters that affect workers in that company, such as changes in working conditions, pay and redundancies, and will negotiate with the company on behalf of all its members. The Union will also carry out regular health and safety inspections.

When a union is recognised, certain members will become Trade Union representatives or shop stewards, and will be specially trained by the Union in employment law and practice and, generally, health and safety. For larger firms there will be several representatives under the general supervision of a senior shop steward or convener.

If a Union member at a firm with Union recognition has a problem at work, his first port of call should be his Union representative. There will generally always be at least one representative on duty at a firm at any one time. As well as general advice, a member has the right to be accompanied by his Union rep at any disciplinary or grievance hearing and will receive advice and assistance in relation to this.

If it is felt that the worker has a claim against the company, for example, for unfair dismissal, then the Union will bring the application to the employment tribunal on his behalf and represent him, or arrange for legal representation, at the hearing.

Although employees at firms with no Union recognition will not have a shop steward on hand at work, they can always call on the services of the local Union office. For example, they will have accredited representatives who can accompany members to disciplinary and grievance hearings.

For advice on joining a Union and contact details see the section on Trades Unions in Part 2.

Other contacts

The Department of Trade and Industry

GOV www.dti.gov.uk/er

This is the Government department responsible for employment matters and the DTI employment relations website contains a wealth of information, for example, on legislation such as the working time regulations, and useful guides, for example, on redundancy payments. The site also contains information about the work of the DTI and gives useful links. The DTI have a number of helpful publications, most of which can be obtained free and ordered online. There is also a contact list online with a telephone number where you can ring for further information on particular topics.

TIGER

GOV
REC
www.tiger.gov.uk/home.htm

TIGER stands for Tailored Interactive Guidance on Employment Rights. This is a government site, part of the DTI site, which aims to guide both employers and employees through employment rights, currently the National Minimum Wage and Maternity Rights. This site is in the process of development and further areas of law are due to be added in due course. The site guides you through a series of questions so you can see how the various rights apply to you. You can also telephone their helpline if you consider that you are not being paid the minimum wage.

National Minimum Wage helpline: 0845 600 0678 (between 8am and 6pm Monday to Friday).

Public Concern at Work (PCAW)

NFP
www.pcaw.co.uk

This is a charity which gives free legal advice to people who have concerns about wrongdoing or malpractice in the workplace. So if, for example, you are worried that your employer might be breaking the law in some way, you can ring the free helpline to discuss the situation with a PCAW legal advisor. All the advisors are qualified lawyers. There is a lot of helpful information on the web-site, including some practical hints.

PCAW also give advice to employers on the Public Interest Disclosure Act and handling staff with concerns in this area.

Suite 306
16 Baldwins Gardens
London EC1N 7RJ
Helpline No: 020 7404 6609
Email: helpline@pcaw.co.uk

OneClickHR

COM
www.oneclickhr.com

This site is aimed at employers but will also be very useful for employees. It has a vast range of information onsite, for example, on long-term sickness absence or health and safety at work. There is also a news service and an interactive area where you can chat online or post messages to a forum. You need to register before using the site, but at the time of writing access to the site is free. There are human resource related services that can be purchased online.

Equality Direct

NFP www.equalitydirect.org.uk

This is an information and advice service for businesses on a range of equality issues such as providing better access for disabled people or equal pay. There is a telephone advice centre and supporting website aimed to help employers resolve management issues, offer information and advice on both good practice and the law and provide information on effective equal opportunities strategies.

Tel: 0845 600 3444

In the following article, David Mead discusses the recent changes in employment law.

The Employment Law Year 2000-2001

Employment law has been developing and expanding over the last few years, and this looks set to continue. This article will consider and highlight four of the important changes over the last 12 months.

Casual and atypical workers

Two recent European Union ('EU') driven developments will change the protection awarded to 'casual' workers and to alleviate some of the drawbacks of not regularly working a 'normal' Monday to Friday 35 hour week.

Regulations made in response to the EU Directive on Part-Time Work came into force in July 2000 and these should benefit the UK's estimated six million part-timers. Unless there is some justification they will prevent employers treating part-time workers differently from full-time workers, for example, as to rates of pay, sick pay, company pensions, maternity/paternity leave, annual leave and access to training.

New regulations on 'fixed-term' work will have a direct effect on the estimated 1.1-1.3 million UK employees who are employed under a series of fixed-term contracts. They will enhance the protection for these employees, most of whom work in the public sector, in three ways. They will:

- protect fixed-term employees from being treated less favourably. For example they cannot have different contractual terms, or be dismissed simply because their job is for a fixed term;

- prevent abuses of fixed-term contracts by limiting successive renewals, so now there can only be four successive fixed term contracts after which the employee will not be on a 'fixed term'; and

- require employers to tell fixed-term employees about permanent vacancies within their organisation.

There have been cases in the European Court of Justice stating that workers will be entitled to their holiday rights from their first day at work, rather than after a 13-week probationary period. Another English case also held that in some circumstances an agency worker can be the employee of the company rather than the agency.

Family-friendly working

The Government either has made or is about to make, in the course of the current Parliament, great changes to the working lives of fathers and mothers.

(1) In April 2001, the Parental Leave Regulations 1999 were changed to allow 13 weeks' leave (per child) for all parents of children aged under five. This followed a TUC-led challenge that claimed that the Government had failed properly to implement the relevant EU Directive. The right is still limited in certain key ways. It is:

- unpaid;
- dependent on an employee having been with the same employer for a year or more, and giving three weeks' notice; and
- available only in one-week chunks, even if only an afternoon is needed.

There is a separate right to unpaid 'reasonable' time off to help dependants in an emergency. This might sometimes be a better means to ensure working parents can cope with domestic crises, as it does not depend on a minimum period of employment.

(2) In June 2001, the Government announced plans to grant a right to request flexible working hours. This could be, for example, a job share or part time work. The duty on employers, however, is merely to give reasonable consideration to the request.

(3) Several changes to maternity (and paternity) rights were announced by the Chancellor, in his March 2001 budget:

- Unpaid maternity leave will be extended by three months to allow a return to work a full year after the birth of a child.

- From April 2003, the weekly rate of statutory maternity pay will be increased and paid for a longer period of time. There is no change to the percentage of salary (90%) being paid for the first six weeks.

- Laws will be passed to give, for the first time, the right to two weeks' paid paternity leave from April 2003. Currently, 'expectant' fathers must rely on the Parental Leave Regulations. However, this is unpaid and therefore it is anticipated that only about 2 per cent of fathers-to-be take up this right. The proposed change still contrasts unfavourably with other European states: Finnish fathers, for example, may take up to six weeks' paid leave.

Human rights in the workplace

The topic of the European Convention for Human Rights and the Human Rights Act (HRA) 1998 is the subject of a separate article in this book, so this article will just highlight a few of the special areas of concern in the employment context.

There have been very few successful challenges to UK working practices at the European Court of Human Rights (and formerly the Commission of Human Rights). For example, a claim that dismissal for refusing to work on Sundays was a breach of Article 9 (right to freedom of religion) was dismissed at an early stage as the Commission placed more reliance on the contractual agreement.

All public sector workers (e.g. those working for government departments or local authorities, and other public authorities) will be able to rely upon the various rights in the human rights legislation, directly against their 'public authority' employer.

It is not known, however, how much private sector employees will benefit. Certainly they will not be able to do so directly. However, all employees will be able to call upon the court - if a case is brought either by or against them - to interpret current UK laws, so as to ensure that their human rights are not restricted or interfered with in an excessive or disproportionate manner.

Very few cases have reached the higher courts under the Human Rights Act since October 2000 and none relating directly to employment. However, the scenarios portrayed below might indicate some of the types of cases for the future:

- Article 14 of the European Convention includes a much wider anti-discrimination provision than current domestic law, so it might be easier for arguments based other than on race, sex and disability to be mounted.

- Unions and their members might look for strength to Article 11 and its guarantee of freedom of association. However, there have been very few successful challenges in this area.

- Similarly, it is unlikely that employees would be able to call upon the European Convention - as an aspect of private life (Article 8) or free expression (Article 10) - to challenge dress codes at work, as such a claim was tried and failed in a case in 1998.

- It might help those who are disciplined at work for behaviour out of working hours - such as was called for by the Prime Minister for violent football fans during the 1998 World Cup in France - as this could be seen as an unreasonable restriction on private life (Article 8).

Surveillance at work

Vetting, security checks, collecting medical data and random or blanket surveillance at work - by monitoring phone calls or email or observation by CCTV - might all breach the Article 8 privacy rights of workers.

Summarising the legal position relating to monitoring and recording calls and email:

- In 1997, the European Court of Human Rights held that monitoring or listening in to calls on the employer's private phone system was a breach of an employee's rights of privacy under Article 8.

- Partly in response and partly as a result of a European Directive, the Regulation of Investigatory Powers Act (RIPA) was passed in July 2000. This legislation makes the interception and monitoring of public and private phone calls, email and the internet both a crime and a civil wrong (leading to damages and/or injunctions). Exceptions are where there is a government warrant or where both parties consent.

- Responding to business concerns about the damage that would be caused if employers could not listen to employees' phone calls unless an employee consented, the Home Secretary issued regulations setting out the grounds on which employers can lawfully monitor their employees' communications, which came into effect in October 2000. These regulations are very wide, effectively providing little restriction on an employer's ability to monitor calls and email.

- Crucially, there is no requirement in the regulations that interceptions should also be proportionate which is important in assessing the lawfulness of interferences with Article 8 privacy rights. So under the Human Rights Act it might be possible for employees to argue that it is unnecessary to monitor the emails of all staff if an employer is really only worried about trade secrets being leaked by a few key personnel.

- Also monitoring in this way will probably have implications under the Data Protection Act 1998. A code of practice is due to be published before the end of 2001.

Conclusion

The future is also likely to witness substantial developments in employment law as a result of EU laws and case decisions. For example:

- greater consultation with employees through works councils;
- more employee protection when a business is sold or transferred as a going concern; and
- greater protection against discrimination on grounds of sexual orientation and age.

Employment law is always developing and changing, and you should always check the current position before taking action.

David Mead

David Mead, formerly a practising solicitor, now lectures at Norwich Law School, University of East Anglia, where he specialises in human rights, public law and employment law.

Family

In this section we look at all the types of problems and situations that would be dealt with in a solicitors' 'family' or matrimonial department. These are basically emergencies/domestic violence, divorce, financial matters, children and co-habitees.

Family mediation is available for all types of family disputes - for more information, see the mediation section below.

When looking for a solicitor for any of the problems discussed below (other than problems regarding care orders involving children), try to find a solicitor who is on the Family Law Panel, or who is a member of the

Solicitors Family Law Association. He will have particular knowledge and experience of family law matters.

As many of the services and contacts listed in this section cover more than one of the types of family problem discussed below, they are all listed together at the end.

Domestic violence

NB: If you are a child (i.e. under 18) suffering from violence at home, see the 'Children' section above.

Sadly, many people (mostly women but also some men) suffer from violence from their partners, and many of them suffer in silence for many years. To a certain extent it is a woman's choice whether she stays with a violent partner or not. However, there are organisations that can help.

If you wish for protection, it is best to get the police involved. They will give support and may be able to bring a charge against your partner where they are not given bail. This will have the same effect as an injunction. Alternatively, they may be given bail conditions, such as not being allowed to return home or contact the victim or witnesses. At the end of a case where the aggressor has been found guilty, the court may make an order protecting the victim. The police can also help you find a solicitor and give information about other services, such as the local women's refuge. It should be mentioned, however, that some victims still find the police unsympathetic.

If you do not wish to involve the police, perhaps because you are worried that a police record will affect your partner's job prospects (and his ability to provide maintenance), you should seek advice from a solicitor. If you are on benefit, or a very low income, you will be eligible for Legal Aid. If you are not eligible for Legal Aid, many solicitors will offer an initial free interview where you can at least get some basic advice. Make sure the solicitor you see specialises in family work.

Divorce and financial matters

When they are separating, married couples generally think of obtaining the actual divorce order from the court. This is fairly straightforward and the forms (and some assistance) can even be obtained online. If there is no dispute over financial matters, then many couples can quite easily deal with this themselves, without using a solicitor. If you are on a low income, you may not even have to pay the court fees - ask the court office about this.

However, most of the problems and difficulties in dealing with divorces occur over dividing up the financial assets between the husband and wife. If there is bad feeling between the parties, this can become acrimonious and difficult to resolve.

If there is likely to be any dispute about the financial settlement, or if you do not know the full extent of your partner's assets income and pension arrangements, it is recommended that, before the divorce is obtained, you see a solicitor who can advise you. However, it is best to try to agree as much as you can with your partner, because solicitors' time costs money - even if you are being advised under Legal Aid, the Legal Services Commission may be able to recoup their costs from money or property which goes to you under any agreement or court order which the solicitor has dealt with for you.

There are **Legal Services Commission booklets** available called 'Divorce and Separation' and 'Sorting things out together'. For information on how to obtain these booklets, see the section on the Legal Services Commission in Part 2.

Children

Legal work involving children divides into three categories - residence (formerly called custody) orders for children where their parents have separated, and problems with access; care orders where children are being taken into care by the local authority; and adoption.

- **Residence/custody/access:** If there is any dispute regarding which parent (or family member or friend) a child will live with, legal advice should be sought from a solicitor. There are frequently problems about access to children by a parent who is not living with the child. Again, it is best to get advice from a family solicitor.

- **Care orders:** If you need legal advice regarding children being taken into care, you should make sure you choose a solicitor who is on the

Children Panel. All Children Panel solicitors are experienced at representing clients at proceedings, and will have received special training. Your social worker will be able to advise you. If there are court proceedings, Legal Aid under the Community Legal Service is non-means tested.

- **Adoption:** To adopt a child you will need to obtain a court order and it is best to have legal help with this. You should ensure that the solicitor you use is familiar with this type of work - a solicitor who is on the Family Law Panel or the Children Panel is best. There are, however, many online sources of information (discussed later in the book) that you can look at before taking any action.

Co-habitees

Many people assume that if a man and a woman live together for a period of time as husband and wife there is a 'common law marriage' and they acquire rights similar to those of married couples. This is not the case. Below are some examples of differences in the rights between married couples and co-habitees:

- Partners do not have any property rights over and above the general law whereas, for example, a wife will be usually entitled to a share in the matrimonial home even if it is in the name of the husband.

- Pensions - co-habitees are not entitled to any pension sharing orders.

- There is no right to maintenance (although you can claim maintenance for children).

- You are not deemed to be your partner's next of kin and therefore are not entitled to be consulted about such things as medical treatment.

- Unmarried fathers do not have any rights over their children unless the mother enters into a parental responsibility order or where a court order has been made. This means, for example, that he is not entitled to receive school reports or medical information about the child.

- Spouses have much greater rights in respect of their partner's property after death.

However, note if you are co-habiting, you will be treated as if you were married by the Department of Social Security so far as the calculation of any benefit is concerned.

Further information regarding problems between unmarried co-habitees can be obtained from some of the contacts below. Also, help can always be obtained from a solicitor who specialises in family law.

Contacts

The Solicitors Family Law Association

SOC www.sfla.co.uk

The website has useful information and fact sheets, and you can find a SFLA solicitor online.

The Child Support Agency Online

GOV www.dss.gov.uk/csa/index.htm

The official site of the Child Support Agency. There is a questions and answers page, and various leaflets you can download.

Child Support Agency Enquiry Line: 08457 133 133
Email: csa-nel@new100.dss.gsi.gov.uk
For general information and advice about child support matters. Calls are normally charged at local rate.

Child Support Agency Advice Durham Legal Services

NFP www.d-l-s98.freeserve.co.uk

This is an independent advice agency that specialises in the Child Support Act legislation. They will give initial telephone advice free of charge. If you then need representation, they will do this for a one-off fee agreed in advice.

PO Box 45
Houghton-le-Spring
Tyne & Wear DH4 5YR
Tel: 0191 521 1123
Fax: 0191 523 8794
After hours mobile: 0771 349 8472
Email: help@csa-advice.fsnet.co.uk

Divorce Online

COM www.divorce-online.co.uk

This is a 'magazine' style website with lots of information about the divorce process, and news items. You can also 'purchase' a divorce online plus other various documents and services.

Divorce Guide UK

COM www.divorceguideuk.co.uk

This is a comprehensive online guide to divorce and family law matters written by Nottingham Solicitors Berryman Shacklock.

Shared Parenting Information Group

NFP www.spig.clara.net

This is a website aimed at helping parents share a role in parenting after separation.

MATCH - Mothers Apart from Their Children

NFP www.match1979.co.uk

MATCH is an organisation for mothers who are not living with their children for whatever reason. By joining MATCH for a modest annual fee, you will receive a quarterly newsletter and receive other benefits. There is an application form online.

Families Need Fathers

NFP www.fnf.org.uk

A very informative website with lots of content, including newsletters and legal articles.

National Council for One Parent Families

Provides information and advice to lone parents and those who work to support them.

255 Kentish Town Road
London NW5 2LX
Tel: 0800 018 5026

Gingerbread

NFP www.gingerbread.org.uk

The support organisation for lone parents in England and Wales. Advice Line - 0800 018 4318 between 10am and 4pm, Monday to Friday.

Women's Aid Federation

NFP www.womensaid.org.uk

Women's Aid is the key national charity in England for women and children experiencing physical, sexual or emotional abuse in their homes. This site has a lot of helpful information and contact details for help organisations and women's refuges.

The Children's Legal Centre

NFP www2.essex.ac.uk/clc

This organisation is concerned with law and policy affecting children and young people. There is a free information service for children and young people and anyone with concerns about them. There is also a legal education advocacy unit.

University of Essex
Wivenhoe Park, Colchester
Essex CO4 3SQ
Advice line: 01206 873820 (Opening times between 10am and 12.30pm and 2pm and 4.30pm, Monday to Friday).
Education Legal Advocacy Unit: 01206 873 966
Fax: 01206 874 026
Email clc@essex.ac.uk

Reunite

NFP www.reunite.org

Reunite is a national charity that deals with the problem of parental child abduction and international custody disputes. You can buy a pack (available in several languages) from them for £3.50, which gives details of legal procedures, and practical steps a parent can take if they fear their children will be abducted. They can also refer you to an international lawyer.

PO Box 24875
London E1 6FR

Advice Line: 020 7375 3440 (Opening times between 10.30am and 5pm, Monday to Friday).
Tel Admin: 020 7375 3441
Fax: 020 7375 3442
Email: use the online form

British Agencies for Adoption and Fostering

NFP www.baaf.org.uk

BAAF, based in London and with offices in Wales, Scotland and England, is the leading membership organisation for agencies and individuals concerned with adoption, fostering and work with children and families. They are also a major publisher, training provider and family finder. The website is excellent with much information and a FAQ page.

Skyline House
200 Union Street
London SE1 0LX
Tel: 020 7593 2023
Fax: 020 7593 2001
Email: membership@baaf.org.uk

Adoption Net

COM www.adoption-net.co.uk

News and information on adoption of children, run by the Derby Telegraph.

NORCAP

NFP The National Organisation for the Counselling of Adoptees and Parents, which offers support, counselling, and intermediary service for tracing relatives.

112 Church Road
Wheatley
Oxfordshire OX33 1LU
Tel: 01865 875 000 (between 10am and 4pm, Monday to Thursday, and between 10am and 12pm, Friday).
Email: enquiries@norcap.org

The Foundling Group

NFP www.foundlings.org

This is a group (under the umbrella group of NORCAP) for adults over the age of 18 who have been abandoned as babies.

Tel: 01865 875 000
Email: info@foundlings.org

In the following article, Marilyn Stowe looks at some key changes in Family Law over the past decade.

Changes for the better - but still more to do

If I had to use one word to sum up changes in family law over the past decade it would be...FAIRER.

The whole process of divorce is infinitely better than it used to be. Changes in legislation have resulted in wives getting a fairer financial deal if their marriages break down and children no longer being treated as assets to be 'owned' by one party or the other. It has also been recognised, and not before time, that fathers have rights too and that it is not always best that children live with their mother. Above all that, the welfare of the child is paramount

There has been a concerted effort on the part of the Government and all the professionals involved to take the bitterness and aggression out of the divorce process. Amicable settlements are now the aim. And to a large degree that is working. It is now very rare to get a 'defended' (i.e. contested) divorce going to court. Mediation and conciliation are the watchwords, words that ten years ago meant very little.

The concept of 'fault' is now largely irrelevant. It is now commonly recognised that there are neither pure saints nor total sinners in relationships. Blame and fault only ever come in now when one party, wishing to prove an irretrievable breakdown to secure an immediate divorce, cites unreasonable behaviour or adultery or, more rarely, in relation to financial disputes.

Divorce - the numbers game

Almost half of all marriages in Britain - two out of every five - now end in divorce. Following the introduction of the Divorce Reform Act of 1969, the annual roll-call of divorces rose from fewer than 80,000 to a peak of 180,000 in 1993.

In 1998, the latest year for which statistics are available, it was running at 160,000. There are divided opinions on whether this reduction is a blip or a new trend, whether it is as a result of fewer marriages or because increasing affluence has taken away one of the most common causes of marital breakdown, financial hardship leading to stress.

The cost of divorce to the national economy, however, is staggering. The Community Legal Service bill for matrimonial and family proceedings is running at around £387 million a year, with the full cost to the public purse of the fall-out from divorce estimated at around £5 billion a year.

Social changes mean that many couples now prefer to merely co-habit rather than go through the financial and emotional pressures of a wedding. By 1992, it was estimated that some 18 per cent of unmarried men aged between 16-59 were living with their partner.

Fathers in divorce

When it comes to exactly whom the children will live with when a marriage breaks down, it seems that fathers are getting a better deal. This has been one of the biggest changes; but is it good enough yet?

At one time, it was almost automatic that, in the event of divorce, the children went to live with their mother. In 1994, for example, 71 per cent of mothers were awarded sole residence. It was just assumed, by judges, social workers and probably society at large, that that was the 'natural' way of things.

Children, particularly young ones, had special and deep psychological bonds with their mothers that it was thought wrong and harmful to break; fathers were seen as breadwinners and not natural home-makers.

The concepts of 'custody' and 'access' disappeared in 1989 with the introduction of The Children Act. These kinds of orders are no longer made. Now the court makes decisions on residence and contact which are not the same concepts at all.

A historic ruling in the Appeal Court in 1991 by Lord Justice Butler-Sloss backed a father's claim that his daughter should live with him and ordered a lower court to reconsider their earlier judgment in favour of the mother. Above all, this case led to a re-examination of how the courts deal with contested residency: the priority is to come to a decision that is in the best interests of the children involved.

It is estimated that anything from 30 per cent to 50 per cent of all fathers lose touch with their children within a couple of years of a divorce, often against their wishes. However, experience shows that if a man puts together a cogent and reasoned argument about why he should have residential care of his children, then the courts are now prepared to look at it in an even-handed way. There is little doubt that the position for fathers today is much better than a decade ago.

The essential principle is that children are not 'owned' by anyone; they are individuals with their own rights and needs. More than ever, courts listen to the opinions of children caught up in relationship breakdowns. However, court is now regarded as the last resort and every avenue is encouraged before a court hearing takes place.

Of course, the best solution to this question is an amicable agreement by both parties as to what is in the best interest of the child. After all, just because two people decide they can no longer live together doesn't turn them into unfit parents overnight!

Sorting the finances

It used to be said that an Englishman's home is his castle and his most important financial asset. These days, however, it's more likely that it's his pension that he guards most jealously, especially when divorce raises the question of sharing the proceeds with his former wife. By and large, we have not yet seen that a wife's pension is as well funded as that of her husband, but in the next ten years we most certainly will, as women will have been at work for lengthy periods.

A husband frequently regards the pension as his reward for a lifetime of work. This is particularly evident in those jobs and careers that demand long and unsociable hours, and that do not pay excessive salaries but offer generous pension provision at the end. This applies to people working within the civil service and the police, for example.

In these cases, and in many others, the husband will often choose to disregard the fact that it was only the support of his wife that enabled him to work so hard. Caring for their home and children was really her 'contribution' to creating the financial safeguard for their life after retirement. She firmly believes she is entitled to an equitable share.

In many cases, after the family home, the pension is the largest financial asset involved in arriving at a settlement. It is a complex and difficult issue. But the whole area of pension-sharing has undergone dramatic change since the introduction of new legislation. The Welfare Reform and Pensions Act 1999 is likely to have a major impact on financial settlements to the positive benefit of women.

Most people expect to pay into their chosen pension schemes all their working lives and for the fund to develop in such a way as to provide for them into their old age. It's just a figure that disappears from the wage packet each month and most people give it no more thought than that until one of two things happens:

(i)   retirement looms and they realise that their pension entitlement is woefully inadequate to sustain their desired lifestyle, particularly as life expectancy increases;

(ii)   the marriage they thought was for life is falling apart and their spouse is demanding a share of the pension.

The most important effect of the new legislation is that it allows for pension sharing straight away. Part of the pension fund (or whatever is agreed or ordered by the court) can be transferred off to the same or a separate fund for the benefit of the spouse, immediately.

This means that both parties can then get on with their lives as the asset that they have been paying into (one directly, the other indirectly), and which continued to bind them together, has been dealt with.

The provisions of the new legislation are bound to have a significant impact on settlements.

There will still, inevitably, be all the problems associated with valuing the pension as part of the divorce settlement. But the new legislation should, at least, make life easier if the asset can be dealt with at the time rather than having to consider the value based on future projections.

One thing, however, is certain. It amounts to a positive step forward for both parties, as it might give the paying party access to more immediate capital, for example, instead of handing over most or all of the equity in the house, this can be traded off for pension provision.

The White v White case that went to the House of Lords in 2000 also resulted in an overall fairer financial settlement, particularly for wives of very rich men who believed they had played a part in the amassing of those assets. This ground-breaking judgment means that:

- where assets exceed need, the surplus is no longer paid over to the husband;

- wives of very rich men divorced after a long marriage will now be entitled to claim parity (although whether they get it remains a moot point);

- there are concerns that this will lead to such men taking elaborate steps to hide their true wealth, hiding assets offshore and making the tracing of funds that much more difficult, adding to costs of divorce and the duration of cases;

- the new ruling will also apply in the case of a divorced husband wanting a half share of a wealthy wife's assets;

- there will be a knock-on effect on other, less asset-rich, cases, where the principles will still apply.

Pre-nuptial agreements

Pre-nuptial (or pre-marital) agreements were once something strictly reserved for the rich and famous. Michael Douglas and Catherine Zeta-Jones signed a pre-nuptial agreement before their lavish wedding in New York. There were even reports of rows regarding the content of the agreement.

It is in the USA where the pre-nuptial agreement is rapidly becoming as important as the engagement ring. The question is whether it has a place in this country and, in particular, for us mere mortals who are not rock superstars or movie-star multi-millionaires.

However, as lifestyles change, they are becoming more and more common. It must be asked though: 'Are they a commonsense agreement between consenting adults or the most unromantic start to a loving relationship that is supposed to be for life?'

Marriage is supposed to be all about showing to the world that you love each other and intend to remain together for the rest of your lives. Even in an age when we have depressingly high divorce statistics, it does seem to me that pre-nuptial agreements are a cold-hearted undermining of this whole concept.

I would go so far as to say that such agreements can actually encourage marital breakdown. How? Well, if part of the agreement includes an instalment arrangement of so much cash per year of marriage, as, reportedly, is the case with Michael Douglas and Catherine Zeta-Jones, then a husband is going to be sorely tempted to throw in the towel at the first sign of fading passion. It will certainly be cheaper!

Pre-nuptial agreements may well have a place in the lives of the Hollywood superstars, where both sides might be phenomenally and independently wealthy and want to protect their financial positions in the event of a breakdown. Tinseltown is hardly the best advertisement for the concept of marriage being for life, so a pre-marriage contract is probably a practical step to ward off the gold-diggers.

And in my practice I have prepared pre-nuptial agreements to cover specific circumstances:

- in a second marriage, where a wife wants to protect the assets she gained from her first marriage and to ensure her children do not lose out in event of the new relationship foundering;

- when a wealthy woman marries a man with considerably fewer financial resources and wants to protect her assets.

At present, however, pre-nuptial agreements are not legally binding here. Our courts are not required to follow the terms as set out in a pre-nuptial agreement. As far as the court is concerned, it is just another piece of paper to be taken into consideration in deciding a fair and reasonable settlement.

There are moves afoot, however, which may see them being given legal standing in the UK; a Government Green Paper on 'Supporting Families' contains a proposal that pre-nuptial agreements and contracts be given legal status.

The proposal is that they should be binding on those who wish to use them. Importantly, however, they would not be binding if the couple go on to have a child or children. In those circumstances, the court would be able to take charge of the financial resources, unfettered by any agreement.

Divorce on demand - the next step

So, much has changed over the past decade. However, I do not believe things have gone far enough. I believe we should have 'divorce on demand'. It seems to me that if proving fault to obtain a divorce encourages parties to look backwards rather than to the future, this outmoded approach should be abandoned as soon as possible. There is no such thing in my opinion as a 'guilt-free' spouse; it takes two to break a marriage rather than one. However, this requires a cultural shift within the legislature. Government has no place in telling people how they should live their lives.

It is wrong to adopt a stance that tries to force a couple back together. There was a failed attempt in the Family Law Act 1996. It should be accepted that if a relationship has gone so wrong that the partners in it are consulting lawyers, then the whole emphasis should be on helping them out of the marriage as quickly and painlessly as possible. Providing of course that the marriage has indeed irretrievably broken down.

Marilyn Stowe

Marilyn Stowe is head of the family law unit at Leeds solicitors Grahame, Stowe, Bateson and Chief Examiner/Chief Assessor of the Law Society's Family Law Panel. She is one of Britain's busiest divorce lawyers, specialising in high wealth cases, particularly those in which major business assets are at stake. She is a regular contributor to radio and television debates and has written for national publications including the Daily Express *and* The Times *as well as for specialist journals. She is also the author of one book,* Divorce: A New Beginning.

Finance, banks & consumer credit problems

see also 'Debt advice' section.

Many people find financial matters confusing and it is often easy for unscrupulous advisors to sell products that are unsuitable. It is also difficult for most people to spot financial irregularities or, if they do, to get these dealt with. However, the organisations listed here may be able to help.

Generally, when taking financial advice, it is best to go to an organisation that is independent. Banks, for example, will normally only sell you their own products, which may not be the best one for you.

If you have a problem with a financial institution, you should first complain to the institution itself. If they are not able to resolve it to your satisfaction, then consider making a complaint to the Financial Ombudsman. The other websites listed below will also have useful information that can help you. They may also have links to other finance related websites.

The Financial Ombudsman

OFF www.financial-ombudsman.org.uk

This is an independent service for consumers with unresolved complaints against financial firms. The Ombudsman can only help you after you have complained initially to the firm concerned, but the website contains some excellent advice on how to make that complaint. If you are unable to resolve matters direct with the firm concerned, then you can complain to the Ombudsman, but your complaint should be made within six months of receiving the letter from the firm giving their final decision on your complaint. The website has a form which you can complete and then print off and send to them. It is a free service.

The Financial Ombudsman Service
South Quay Plaza
183 Marsh Wall
London E14 9SR

Tel for banking-related complaints: 0845 766 0902
Tel for insurance-related complaints: 0845 600 6666
Tel for personal investment complaints: 020 7216 0016
Switchboard: 020 7964 1000
Main fax: 020 7964 1001
Email: enquiries@financial-ombudsman.org.uk

The Financial Services Authority

OFF www.fsa.gov.uk

The Financial Services Authority is an independent body that regulates the financial services industry in the UK. The website has a useful consumer section where consumer rights in the finance industry are explained. You can also check the FSA's Central Register of firms currently or formerly authorised to carry on investment business in the UK, which is available online. This will enable you to check a firm before doing business with it. If you cannot access the list online, you can also make telephone or postal enquiries.

25 The North Colonnade
Canary Wharf
London E14 5HS
Consumer helpline: 0845 606 1234
Fax: 020 7676 1099
Email: consumerhelp@fsa.gov.uk

The Finance Industry Standards Association

OFF www.fisa.co.uk

This organisation sets standards for the credit brokers for secured loans. The site sets out the FISA code of practice and other information including the borrower information guide which can be downloaded.

Parrys Court
Northgate, Sleaford
Lincolnshire NG34 7BN
Tel: 01529 305 698
Fax: 01529 414 313

Credit reference agencies

These are organisations that hold information about all of us and which can be consulted by banks, building societies and other organisations to find out information about you before lending you money or granting you credit. The two agencies below are the main credit reference agencies. You have the right to obtain copies of your entries from them (upon payment of a small fee) and to ask them to correct any inaccuracies in their records. If you find that you are being refused credit, it is important that you check your details in this way, just in case someone is using your name to run up credit. For example, if your credit cards are stolen, this may happen. The websites are very helpful and will guide you through the process of obtaining your file details.

Experian Limited

COM www.experian.co.uk
Consumer Help Service
PO Box 8000
Nottingham NG1 5GX
Tel: 0115 958 1111
Fax: 0115 976 8866
Email: Corporate.communications@uk.experian.com

Equifax Europe Ltd

COM www.equifax.co.uk
Consumer Affairs Department
PO Box 3001
Erskine House
1A North Avenue
Glasgow G81 2DT
Tel: 0141 951 1100
Fax: 0141 951 2300
Email: moreinfo.uk@equifax.com

Also you can find out about your own credit rating by contacting:

The Credit File Advice Centre

PO Box 3001
Glasgow G81 2DT

Foreign law

This book is mainly aimed at the English or Welsh reader with some Scottish related information. There may, however, be times when the general reader needs some information on foreign law. However, it is impossible in a book of this size to do anything other than to indicate how you can go about trying to find a suitable source of information.

The best place to look for information on any foreign law is the internet, and the best place to start is Delia Venables's site. See her page headed 'Legal Sites and Resources in Other Countries', and follow her mystery tour of the best legal resources worldwide.

If you wish to find a foreign lawyer, there are some online legal directories, although they tend to concentrate on commercial firms rather than the smaller firms, which would normally act for individuals. You may also find a firm through some of the international sites you will find on Delia Venables's foreign links pages.

Also, set out below is some information on the Notaries Society that also deals with foreign law.

Martindale Hubbell

COM
FOR www.martindale.com

A large American directory that has links to international firms worldwide.

The Notaries Society

SOC www.thenotariessociety.org.uk

Notaries are a small but ancient profession. They commonly deal with the following:

- preparing and witnessing powers of attorney for use overseas;
- dealing with purchase or sale of land and property abroad;
- providing documents to deal with the administration of the estate of people who are abroad, or owning property abroad;
- authenticating personal documents and information for immigration or emigration purposes, or to apply for work abroad.

The Society's website has general information about notaries, and a search facility that will help you find a notary near you.

Holidays

The main problems generally encountered by people on holidays are inaccurate descriptions in holiday brochures and personal injuries suffered abroad. Further information relating to these can also be found in the 'Consumer' and 'Accidents' sections. Remember, that if you have real problems while you are abroad, you can always contact the local British diplomatic mission for help.

If you suffer loss as a result of your problems, compensation can usually be claimed from your holiday insurance. Also, do not forget that if you pay for all or part of your holiday by credit card, you may be able to make a claim against the card company as well as the holiday company. In addition, you may be covered by free insurance from your credit card provider. There may be other insurance policies you hold which may help. It is always worth making an enquiry.

Here is a number of organisations and useful websites:

The Foreign and Commonwealth Office Travel Overseas

GOV
REC www.fco.gov.uk/travel

These pages contain very useful information for travellers, and you can also find specific information on the country you are travelling to. It is worth checking out this site before you go. See also:

The Consumer Gateway

GOV www.consumer.gov.uk

This site is referred to in the consumer section above but is repeated here as it has useful information on holidays.

UK Passport Agency

GOV www.ukpa.gov.uk

This site provides information on applying for UK passports. There is an online form that can be completed and printed off. There is also an 'application tracker' facility where you can email the agency if you have already applied but suddenly need your passport urgently and they will advise you how long the application will take.

National tel enquiry line: 0870 521 0410
This national call centre provides a single point of contact for all telephone callers and is available 24 hours a day, seven days a week.

Association of British Travel Agents (ABTA)

COM
SOC

www.abtanet.com

This is the main organisation for travel agents which is best known for its arbitration scheme. The website is rather sparse but you can contact the company to make enquiries.

68-71 Newman Street
London W1T 3AH
Tel: 020 7637 2444
Fax: 020 7637 0713

There is a general travel and tourism information line, 0901 201 5050 (UK callers only), open during office hours only. Calls, however, are charged at 50p per minute.

If the company you have booked with has ceased trading, telephone 020 7307 2041 or email claims@abta.co.uk.

Association of Independent Tour Operators (AITO)

If your travel company is not a member of ABTA it may be a member of AITO. They also run an arbitration scheme. Contact details are as follows:

The AITO Independent Dispute Settlement Service
Ron Wheal Associates
Eskdale
47 Aldenham Avenue
Radlett
Herts WD7 8HZ
Tel: 01923 856 615

The Air Transport Users Council

OFF www.auc.org.uk

This is the consumer watchdog for the airline industry. They can advise travellers on their rights and sometimes take up individual cases to obtain redress for passengers who have been badly treated. Their website has a lot of useful information for travellers.

CAA House
45-59 Kingsway
London WC2B 6TE
Advice line tel: 020 7240 6061 (Weekdays 2-5pm)
Fax: 020 7240 7071

Holidaycomplaint.com

COM www.holidaycomplaint.com

This is a website set up to create a database of complaints about holidays and holiday companies. There is also some helpful guidance on making a complaint.

Travel Law

ACC tlc.unn.ac.uk/index.htm

This is a site from the University of Northumbria. It is primarily aimed at delegates to its travel courses, but it has a useful section on travel law material such as links to the various codes in the travel industry.

Housing & homelessness - see
'Property law and housing' section.

Human rights, discrimination & public law

This is a very large and important area of law that encompasses many different types of problem. The Human Rights Act 2000 has been passed recently which has incorporated many new rights into English law - see the article by Liberty below.

As well as the Human Rights Act, there are a number of other Acts which fall into this area, such as the anti-discrimination legislation and the Data Protection Act. The anti-discrimination legalisation is perhaps most commonly used to claim compensation for discrimination at work. However, it can also be used in other circumstances, such as at school or college.

The Data Protection Act regulates the information people can hold about you, and all organisations that hold such information now have to register with the Office of the Information Commission (formerly the Data Protection Commissioner). For further information, see the website on page 134.

Public law is a set of legal principles that governs the exercise of power by public authorities. The remedies available include procedures by which people can challenge the fairness or legality of their decisions. This area of law is not well known and if you feel you have a case, it is best to get advice from a solicitor or other practitioner familiar with this area of work. This is probably best done via the Just Ask website.

There are **Legal Services Commission booklets** on the Human Rights Act, racial discrimination, equal opportunities and rights for people with disabilities. For information on how to obtain these leaflets, see the section on the Legal Services Commission in Part 2.

The Home Office Human Rights Unit

GOV www.homeoffice.gov.uk/hract/hramenu.htm

This is part of the Home Office site and contains the usual mix of press releases, articles, speeches and reports. Follow the 'guidance' link for a very clear introduction to human rights and a study guide.

The Scottish Human Rights Trust

www.scotrights.org

NFP The trust is the educational arm of the Scottish Human Rights Centre. It has much information about human rights, with particular reference to Scotland.

Liberty

www.liberty-human-rights.org.uk

Liberty is an independent human rights organisation that works to defend and extend rights and freedoms in England and Wales. Founded in 1934, it is the largest organisation of its kind in Europe and is democratically run. The website is huge and includes news and details of its campaigning work, training and other events. There is also a teaching pack for schools that can be downloaded from the site. Liberty will give free advice either by telephone or post on Human Rights matters. You can also join Liberty and will receive a quarterly newsletter.

Liberty
21 Tabard Street
London SE1 4LAX
Legal Advice Line - 020 7378 8659 open between 6pm and 8pm, Monday and Thursday evening, 12.30pm and 2.30pm, Wednesday lunchtime.
Email: Info@liberty-human-rights.org.uk

Commission for Racial Equality

www.cre.gov.uk

The Commission for Racial Equality is a publicly funded, non-governmental body set up under the Race Relations Act 1976 to tackle racial discrimination and promote racial equality. It works in the public and private sectors to encourage fair treatment and to promote equal opportunities for everyone, regardless of their race, colour, nationality, or national or ethnic origin. It can assist people with complaints about racial harassment, discrimination or abuse, conduct formal investigations and take legal action where necessary. There are several CRE offices but initial enquiries can be made at the London Head Office.

Elliot House
10-12 Allington Street
London SW1E 5EH
Tel: 020 7932 5205
Fax: 0207 630 7605
Email: info@cre.gov.uk

Harassment Law

COM www.harassment-law.co.ukmsindex.htm

This is the website of Neil Addison, a barrister who specialises in this area of law. His website aims to help the victims of harassment and those wrongly accused of it. It is a comprehensive site with useful links.

Data Protection

GOV www.dataprotection.gov.uk

The Data Protection Act now affects all our lives. To find out more about your rights and obligations under the Act, visit this comprehensive website. For general advice, follow the 'principles of data protection' link. You can also search the Data Protection Register online.

Data Protection Commissioner
Wycliffe House
Water Lane
Wilmslow
Cheshire SK9 5AF
Information line: 01625 545 745
Email: mail@dataprotection.gov.uk

The Public Law Project

NFP www.publiclawproject.org.uk

The Public Law Project (PLP) is an independent, national legal charity that aims to improve access to public law remedies for those whose access is restricted by poverty, discrimination or other similar barriers. Its services are aimed mainly at legal professionals and advisors. However, those interested in this area of law will find the website very informative. The organisation does not offer an advice service to the general public and therefore other contact details are not given here.

In the following article, Liberty, an organisation which protects civil liberties, discusses the Human Rights Act in detail and how to use it to one's benefit.

The Human Rights Act 1998

The Human Rights Act 1998 (the 'Act') came into effect on 2 October 2000. It is an extremely important piece of legislation, which incorporates the European Convention on Human Rights (the 'Convention') into the law of the United Kingdom.

The European Convention on Human Rights

The Convention was drawn up at the end of the Second World War. Its provisions aim to protect fundamental human rights, including the right to life, freedom from torture, freedom from arbitrary arrest, the right to a fair trial, the right to privacy, freedom of religion, freedom of expression, and freedom of assembly and association. The Convention has been extended through the adoption of protocols that set out additional rights (these include the right to education and the right to free elections). The United Kingdom has not signed up to all of these protocols. It also has not incorporated article 13 of the Convention, which provides that people whose rights under the Convention have been breached should have an effective means of seeking redress (the Government took the view that the Human Rights Act itself provided this). The rights set out in the Convention and protocols which have been incorporated into UK law are referred to as 'Convention rights'.

Introducing Convention rights into UK law

Before the introduction of the Act, people in the UK could only enforce their Convention rights by making an application to the European Court of Human Rights. This is a lengthy and complex process. Since 2 October 2000, individuals have had a right of redress in the UK courts. In broad terms, the Act gives effect to Convention rights in three ways:

- all legislation must be interpreted, wherever possible, in a way that will uphold and protect Convention rights;

- public authorities (including the courts) must act in compliance with Convention rights, unless they are prevented from doing so by legislation; and

- any new legislation must be drawn up with regard to the Convention to ensure it respects Convention rights, and any current legislation which is not compatible with the Convention can be amended under a 'fast track' procedure.

Issuing proceedings under the Human Rights Act

Where a public authority acts in a way that is incompatible with Convention rights (this includes a failure to act), a person who is a 'victim' can issue proceedings under the Act. For the purposes of the Act a 'victim' is someone who is actually and directly affected by the act or omission that he or she alleges has breached his or her Convention rights, or someone who is at risk of being directly affected.

It is important to note that proceedings can only be issued in respect of acts or omissions of public authorities (such as government departments, local councils, the police, the Prison Service and the Benefits Agency), or 'quasi-public authorities'. Quasi-public authorities are bodies that do not solely perform public functions, and include bodies such as Railtrack, housing associations, the BBC and private security firms managing contracted out prisons. These bodies will only be liable under the Act where they are carrying out public functions, rather than when acting in their private capacity such as, for example, in employment matters. However, the Act will be significant in all cases, as it requires the courts to act in compliance with Convention rights, and to interpret legislation in accordance with those rights.

Proceedings must be issued within one year of the date on which the alleged violation of the Convention right occurs. The Act can also be used in judicial review proceedings. Judicial review proceedings are proceedings where a judge is asked to consider the legality of a decision or act by a public authority or the validity of the basis on which a decision has been made. The Act will allow a claimant to argue that a public authority has acted unlawfully by acting in breach of Convention rights. Judicial review proceedings must be commenced promptly and at the latest within three months of the relevant act or decision being challenged.

Remedies available under the Human Rights Act

Under the Act, a court can grant any remedy within its powers that it considers appropriate given the particular circumstances of the case. Such remedies include compensation, declarations that an act is unlawful and injunctions.

Where a court cannot construe a piece of legislation so as to comply with the Human Rights Act, it will be forced to make a declaration of incompatibility. Declarations of incompatibility will serve to raise public awareness of the relevant issue and will put pressure on the Government to implement changes to the law, but will not provide individuals with an immediate remedy.

Where an individual is dissatisfied with a declaration of incompatibility, or a court's finding that no violation of Convention Rights has occurred, they will be able to make an application to the European Court of Human Rights, which has the power to award compensation.

The Articles of the Human Rights Act in detail

Absolute rights and qualified rights

Certain rights, such as the prohibition on torture, are absolute rights, and cannot be restricted even in times of war or other public emergencies. Other rights, such as the right to privacy, are qualified rights which can be interfered with in certain circumstances. Any interference must be lawful, necessary in a democratic society and proportionate to the aim it seeks to achieve. The permitted aims are set out in the text of the articles and include the prevention of disorder or crime, the protection of the rights and freedoms of others, and the protection of public order.

Article 2: Right to life

This article imposes a duty on public authorities not to deprive anyone of his or her right to life through the use of lethal force, and to take reasonable steps to protect life. For example, the police must take steps to protect someone whose life is being threatened by another. Article 2 also requires any investigation of a death caused by a public body to be independent and effective.

Under Article 2, a public authority can justify taking someone's life in three situations: where they are protecting someone else from unlawful violence, where they are trying to arrest someone or prevent someone from escaping from custody, or where they are trying to stop a riot occurring. However, the public authority will have to show that the force used was no more than was absolutely necessary in the circumstances.

Article 3: Prohibition of torture

This article provides that no one shall be tortured, or punished or treated in a way that is inhumane or degrading. The European Court of Human Rights has defined torture as deliberate inhumane treatment causing very serious and cruel suffering. Inhumane treatment or punishment is punishment that causes intense physical and mental suffering, whilst degrading treatment or punishment is that which causes the victim to feel fear, anguish and inferiority, which is capable of humiliating and debasing the victim.

This article has been used to challenge a local authority's failure to safeguard adequately the welfare of children, and the degrading treatment of a female transsexual.

Article 4: Prohibition of slavery and forced labour

This article prohibits slavery and forced or compulsory labour. It does not apply to prisoners, military service, civil obligations or in emergencies.

Article 5: Right to liberty and security

Article 5 guarantees liberty and security of the person. It also provides a set of procedural rights for people who are detained, such as the requirement that proceedings are brought quickly, and that people are told the reason for their arrest in a language they understand. Any detention must be prescribed by law and must be for one of the purposes set out in Article 5; these purposes include imprisoning a person when he or she has been convicted of an offence; preventing someone from committing a crime; deporting or extraditing someone; and protecting someone who is mentally ill, an alcoholic or a drug addict. Article 5 also gives some people who are detained (for example, compulsory patients in a mental hospital or discretionary life prisoners) the right to have a court or tribunal reconsider the reasons for their detention from time to time.

Article 6: Right to a fair trial

Article 6 provides that everyone has the right to a fair trial, and sets standards that both civil and criminal proceedings must meet. It provides that trials should be held within a reasonable time before an independent judge, and should be held in public (other than in certain exceptional circumstances). In addition, judges' decisions should be made public and reasons for those decisions should be given.

In criminal proceedings, the following additional rights are protected: the right to be presumed innocent until proven guilty, the right for an accused to be told at an early stage what he or she is accused of, the right to remain silent, the right to be granted enough time to prepare a defence, the right to be granted public funding for a lawyer, the right for an individual to be present at his or her own trial, the right for an individual to put forward his or her own case, the right to question key witnesses and to call witnesses, and the right to an interpreter where necessary.

Article 7: No punishment without law

This article prohibits the use of criminal penalties that are not prescribed by law; it prohibits the use of retrospective or arbitrary criminal penalties. It also requires that the law is sufficiently clear and certain to allow people to know whether or not they are acting lawfully.

Article 8: The right to respect for private and family life

This article protects respect for a person's private life, family life, home and correspondence. The right includes privacy of communications, privacy of the home and office, protection from corporal punishment and physical abuse, protection from environmental pollution, and protection from arbitrary interference by the state in an individual's private sexual activities.

The right to respect for private and family life is a qualified right and interference with this right can be justified in certain circumstances. For example, the use of telephone bugging devices might be justified to prevent crime, despite such devices interfering with an individual's right to privacy.

Article 9: Freedom of thought, conscience and religion

This article protects freedom of thought, conscience and religion; it extends to beliefs such as veganism and pacificism as well as more conventional religious beliefs. The article also protects the right to manifest a religion or belief. The right to manifest a religion or belief is a qualified right, and as such can be interfered with in certain circumstances.

Article 10: Freedom of expression

This article protects freedom of expression; it allows people to express themselves freely by any means. It guarantees an individual's right to hold opinions and to receive and impart information.

Again, this is a qualified right; restrictions on freedom of expression have been imposed on journalists to prevent them from interfering with another person's right to life.

Article 11: Freedom of assembly and association

Article 11 protects the right to peaceful protest by holding meetings and demonstrations, the right to associate with others, and the right to form and join trade unions and other similar bodies.

The right to freedom of assembly and association is a qualified right. Prohibitions on the holding of public assemblies might be justified to prevent disorder and crime.

Article 12: Right to marry and found a family

This article provides men and women with the right to marry once when they reach the lawful age; it also provides them with the right to found a family. The right does not apply to same sex or transgender couples.

Article 14: Prohibition on discrimination

Article 14 does not provide a general right to protection from discrimination; rather it will only apply in conjunction with one of the other Convention rights. For example, Article 14 has been raised with Article 8 (the right to a private life) to challenge the criminalisation of homosexual activity in Northern Ireland.

The non-exhaustive grounds of discrimination identified in the article are: sex, race, colour, language, religion, political or other opinion, national or social origin, association with a national minority, property, birth or other status. The category 'other status' has been used to cover discrimination suffered by people who are homosexual, illegitimate, unmarried or a prisoner.

Article 1 of Protocol 1: Right to property

This article guarantees the right to peaceful enjoyment of possessions, but also preserves the right of the state to interfere with this right where the law allows it to do so, and it is in the public interest. The term 'property' is very broad and encompasses shares, pensions and welfare benefits that a person has contributed to through national insurance payments.

Article 2 of Protocol 1: Right to education

This article enshrines the right of access to education, and requires the state to respect the parents' philosophical and religious convictions. The article has been used successfully by parents opposed on principle to corporal punishment to challenge the use of corporal punishment in state schools.

Article 3 of Protocol 1: Right to free elections

This article requires the state to hold elections at reasonable intervals and by secret ballot. It grants people the right to vote or to stand in elections, although certain restrictions may be permissible.

Articles 1 and 2 of Protocol 6: Abolition of the death penalty

This protocol abolishes the use of the death penalty in peacetime, but allows the state to use this penalty during war, or when there is an imminent threat of war.

Liberty

Liberty is an independent non-governmental organisation which works to protect civil liberties and promote human rights in England and Wales. One of the leading organisations of its kind in Europe, with a large public membership, it takes test cases through the English and European courts and lobbies extensively in Parliament and the media on key human rights issues.

Immigration & nationality

This is a large, important, but highly specialised area of practice. There are three main areas of law and practice covered:

1. Immigration - the regulation of foreign nationals coming to the UK to live.

2. Nationality - the law relating to foreign nationals obtaining British nationality.

3. Asylum - allowing genuine refugees from trouble spots in the world, or those whose lives may be threatened by reason of political, social or religious conviction, to stay in this country.

Within these fields are included family immigration, for example, when British nationals marry abroad and wish to bring their spouse to live in the UK, and employment related immigration when people have to obtain a work permit to live and work in the UK.

If you are refused entry to the UK or are refused permission to remain in the country, you may be able to appeal to the Immigration Appellate Authority. However, if an appeal is possible the Home Office will normally tell you this.

Obtaining advice: A considerable amount of information can be found from the organisations below, in particular the Home Office and Nationality Directorate website. However, if you have an immigration related problem, it is best to obtain legal advice from a specialist.

In this case, it is best to contact either a qualified solicitor or barrister experienced in this field, or a practitioner who is licensed by the Office of the Immigration Service Commissioner. Be careful whom you instruct - if someone offering their services approaches you, make sure that they have the necessary training and experience. When instructing solicitors, be warned that most solicitors have no, or very little, knowledge of immigration matters. There are relatively few solicitors specialising in immigration - the majority of these tend to practise in firms close to the major airports, such as Heathrow.

The new Human Rights legislation is now important in various areas of immigration and nationality law, for example, the right to family life and privacy, the right to life and the right not to be subjected to inhuman and degrading treatment. These all address issues that are important, for example, in asylum law, and must be taken into account when considering any immigration claim.

There is a **Legal Services Commission booklet** on claiming asylum. For information on how to obtain these leaflets, see the section on the Legal Services Commission in Part 2.

Office of the Immigration Service Commissioner (OISC)

GOV www.oisc.gov.uk

Newly established for regulating immigration advisors who are non-qualified lawyers. At the time of writing, the website was still under construction. However, you can search online to find a registered organisation near to you. There is also information on the code of standards and about making a complaint about a registered practitioner.

6th Floor, Fleetbank House
2-6 Salisbury Square
London EC4Y 8JX
Tel: 020 7211 1500
Fax: 020 7211 1553

The Home Office Immigration and Nationality Directorate

GOV
REC www.ind.homeoffice.gov.uk

This is an extremely helpful and comprehensive website with information about getting legal advice, online application forms, appeals, asylum, employers' information, and information for tourism, as well as news and other information. There are separate sections on staying in the UK and applying for British Nationality. This is a good place to start when making enquiries about all immigration and nationality matters. Further information can be obtained from the addresses and telephone numbers on the following page:

For immigration enquiries, contact:

Immigration & Nationality Directorate
Block C, Whitgift Centre
Wellesley Road
Croydon CR9 1AT
Tel: 0870 606 7766

For nationality general enquiries or leaflets, contact:

Home Office IND
Immigration & Nationality Policy Directorate
3rd Floor, India Buildings
Water Street
Liverpool L2 0QN
Tel. 0151 237 5200

For enquiries about asylum support, contact:

The National Asylum Support Service
Tel: 0845 602 1739
Fax: 0845 601 1143

For enquiries about employment related immigration contact:

The Department of Trade and Industry
Work Permit UK
Porter Brook House
W5 Moorfoot
Sheffield S1 4PQ
Tel: 0114 259 4425
Fax: 0114 275 3275

Work Permit Applications hotline: 0117 924 4730

The Joint Entry Clearance Unit (JECU)

GOV   www.fco.gov.uk/ukvisas

This organisation runs the UK's pre-entry control through Visa and Consular Officers operating across British Embassies and High Commissions throughout the world. For more information on visas generally, see the website.

89 Albert Embankment
London SE1 7TP
Tel: 020 7238 3858
Fax: 020 7238 3759/3761
Email: visa.foruk@jecu.mail.fco.gov.uk

The Immigration Advisory Service

OFF   www.iasuk.org

The IAS provides assistance, free of charge, to people who have problems with British Immigration Controls, and deals extensively with refugees.

3rd Floor, County House
190 Great Dover Street
London SE1 4YB
24 hour information support line: 020 7378 9191
Support for immigrants in detention: 0800 435 427

The Refugee Council

NFP www.refugeecouncil.org.uk

The Refugee Council is the largest organisation in the UK working with asylum seekers and refugees. They give help and support to asylum seekers and work with refugees and refugee community organisations. There is a considerable amount of information on the website in the 'info centre', together with information about their publications, many of which can be ordered online.

Head Office
3 Bondway
London SW8 1SJ
Advice line: 020 7346 6777 open between 10am and 4pm, Monday to Friday.
Tel: 020 7820 3000
Fax: 020 7582 9929
Email: info@refugeecouncil.org.uk

The Immigration Index

COM www.immigrationindex.org

This is a useful index to websites and articles on all aspects of immigration and related issues.

Immigration News

COM www.asylum.immigrationnews.org

An index with links to new items about immigration and related matters.

Nic Nicol

COM www.niknicol.co.ukindex.html

This is a barrister's site with a section on asylum seeker support. There is a lot of useful information including links to important legislation.

Internet law

This is the law relating to the internet itself, for example, regarding domain names, ecommerce, privacy, etc. There are several sites giving information but they are often very technical and aimed more at legal and internet professionals. Weblaw has some helpful articles, as do the government sites.

Perhaps the area of law most relevant to the consumer are the Distance Selling Regulations. You will find information on these on several of the government sites, such as the Office of Fair Trading or the DTI site.

Weblaw

COM   www.weblaw.co.uk

A useful website from Sprecher Grier Halberstam Solicitors that has helpful articles on many aspects of internet law and the provision of services over the internet.

Law Pack Publishing

COM   www.lawpack.co.uk

Law Pack Publishing produces various guides to the internet, including *The Legal Guide to Online Business* by specialist solicitor Susan Singleton. This book discusses legal issues such as domain names, trade marks, international jurisdictions, credit card transactions, partnerships, alliances, online contracts, employee email, cyber crimes and internet policies. Template documents are included.

Mediation & alternative dispute resolution (ADR)

Mediation is resolving disputes by conciliation rather than by way of a formal trial in the law courts or a tribunal. Probably the best-known organisation that does this is ACAS - see the employment section.

Many of the organisations offering mediation and ADR services are aimed at business disputes and are therefore not included here. An up to date list of their websites, and also further information on mediation and ADR itself, can be found on Delia Venables' site.

Mediation is becoming increasingly important in family disputes and some well-known organisations are listed below which will give further information. However, mediation can also be used in other situations, such as for neighbour disputes. For further information on this, see the Mediation UK link below.

There is a **Legal Services Commission booklet** on family mediation called 'Sorting things out together'. For information on how to obtain these leaflets, see the section on the Legal Services Commission in Part 2.

Mediation UK

NFP www.mediationuk.org.uk

Mediation UK is a national charity that represents and supports mediation within local communities. It is at the hub of a national network of mediation services that usually specialise in one or more areas of mediation. These areas can involve anything from resolving conflicts between neighbours or amongst school children, to mediating between victims of crime and their offenders. Mediation UK also supports constructive conflict resolution within institutions such as the workplace, and specific sectors such as the health service. The website has information on mediation in general and in particular on neighbour mediation, victim offender mediation and school peer mediation. You can also use the website to find a mediator near to you.

Alexander House
Telephone Avenue
Bristol BS1 4BS
Tel: 0117 904 6661
Fax: 0117 904 3331
Email: enquiry@mediationuk.org.uk

National Family Mediation

NFP www.nfm.u-net.com

A registered charity that has a network of over 60 local not-for-profit Family Mediation Services in England and Wales offering help to couples, married or unmarried, who are in the process of separation and divorce. NFM mediators help clients to reach joint decisions about the issues associated with their separation - children, finance and property. Several NFM services also provide specialist services for children. The website has information about the services offered and you can locate the officer nearest to you.

9 Tavistock Place
London WC1H 9SN

The UK College of Family Mediators

OFF www.ukcfm.co.uk

One area where mediation is being encouraged is family mediation, particularly if you are seeking Legal Aid. The UK College of Family Mediators is the professional standards-setting watchdog and public information-providing body for family mediation in England, Scotland, Wales and Northern Ireland. The website shows how family mediation works and gives information on finding a mediator.

24-32 Stephenson Way
London NW1 2HX
Tel: 020 7391 9162 between 9am and 5pm, Monday-Friday.
Email: info@ukcfm.co.uk

Relate

NFP www.relate.org.uk

A national registered charity that provides counselling, sex therapy, relationship education and training to support couple and family relationships throughout life. The website gives information about their services and you can read their fact sheets online.

Herbert Gray College
Little Church Street
Rugby
Warwickshire CV21 3AP
Tel: 01788 573 241
Email: enquiries@national.relate.org.uk

Mental health

Under the Mental Health Act 1983 patients can, if they are mentally disordered, be prescribed treatment and be admitted to hospital against their will.

If you wish for advice and assistance by a solicitor, you should choose one who is a member of the Mental Health Review Tribunal Panel who will have experience in this type of work. You can get a list of solicitors on the panel from the Law Society (Tel: 0870 606 2500) and on the internet (you will have to find the section on solicitors' panels on www.solicitors-online.com and it is in the section on the Mental Health Review Tribunal). Alternatively, you can do a search for solicitors specialising in Mental Health work on the Solicitors Online website or the Just Ask website.

Mark Walton

COM www.markwalton.net

This is a useful guide to the Mental Health Act with clear, easy to read descriptions of the Act, the various sections, and your rights. This is a good place to start if you want to understand the Mental Health Act. There are also articles and news items, plus a section on human rights.

Patents, trademark law & intellectual copyright

This area of law concerns the protection of rights and ownership of non-physical things such as music, books, trademarks, inventions and the like. It is a complex area of law. However, the websites mentioned later in this section will provide useful information and help. If you have a legal problem in this area of law and wish to instruct a solicitor, you should look for a specialist, as general practitioners will not normally be able to help. Most specialists are in the large city firms, although there are some small niche practices. Do not expect a good solicitor in this field to be cheap!

Intellectual Property

GOV
REC www.intellectual-property.gov.uk

This is a government site that explains the concepts of intellectual property, copyright, patents and trademarks. This is a good starting point if you wish to understand this complex area.

The UK Patent Office

GOV   www.patent.gov.uk

This is a useful site with much information, explaining the services of the Patent Office. There is also a Central Enquiry Unit which can answer your queries.

Main Office Address:
The Patent Office
Concept House
Cardiff Road
Newport
South Wales NP10 8QQ

Tel: The Central Enquiry Unit - 0845 950 0505. Phone lines are open between 9am and 5pm, Monday to Friday with the exception of national holidays.
Fax: 01633 813 600
Email: enquiries@patent.gov.uk

Copyright Vault Ltd

COM   www.copyrightvault.com

This company offers musicians, authors, programmers and artists an affordable service to register their copyright. You can do this by sending a copy of your work to them (plus a payment) which they store, so you can prove your copyrights at a future date should you need to. They can also refer you to a solicitor for some initial free advice. The website contains some basic information on copyright and links.

2nd Floor, Cunard Building
Liverpool L3 1DS

Pipers Virtual Intellectual Property Library

COM   www.piperpat.co.nz
FOR   Pipers are a firm of attorneys in New Zealand. This site is an international resource with links to patent attorneys worldwide.

Property law & housing

There is a lot of law relating to property and housing matters, much of it difficult for the layperson to understand. The ordinary person will normally come into contact with property law either when he is buying or selling his own property (known as conveyancing) or when renting a property to live in. Some people will be evicted or be homeless for some other reason and need advice. People running their own businesses may become involved in renting business properties. Additionally, some people will become involved in the planning legislation, either in connection with their own or neighbouring properties.

There are **Community Legal Services booklets** available on 'Losing your home', 'Renting and letting', and 'Buying and selling property'. For details on how to obtain these, see the 'Community Legal Service' section in Part 2.

Conveyancing

When buying and selling property (and long leases are included here), there is a number of legal formalities that need to be carried out; these are known collectively as conveyancing, after the 'conveyance', the document which transfers legal ownership of land from one person to another. Although a person can carry out his own conveyancing, it is normal to have this work done either by a solicitor or (since 1987) a licensed conveyancer.

Many people resent paying for conveyancing and try to obtain the cheapest quote possible for the work. However, the purchase of a house or flat is one of the most expensive transactions most people will ever do, and it makes sense to ensure that the legal title is checked thoroughly and the formalities carried out in a proper way. If a mistake occurs at this stage, for example, if the wrong boundary line is put on the conveyance plan, or if the local searches are not checked properly, you may find that your neighbours are entitled to occupy part of what you thought was your garden or that a motorway is to be built close to your house. Any such problems will inevitably cause you much inconvenience, distress and expense, and, even if you do eventually obtain compensation, will be something you could well do without. It is surely worth using an experienced solicitor or licensed conveyancer and paying a proper fee to ensure that these matters are thoroughly checked. This is particularly important if you are buying a house in the country, unregistered land or if there is anything unusual about the property or its location.

Most firms of solicitors will have a conveyancing department. If you wish to use a licensed conveyancer, a list can be obtained from the Council for Licensed Conveyancers on 01245 349 599 (see also the information on Licensed Conveyancers in Part 2), or your local Council, CAB or Housing Information Centre. Be wary of very cheap quotes for conveyancing work. Can they really afford to do a proper job for that price?

Solicitors and licensed conveyancers showing the transaction logo have all agreed to adopt the Law Society's national transaction protocol.

There is a **Legal Services Commission booklet** on buying and selling property. For information on how to obtain these leaflets, see the section on the Legal Services Commission in Part 2.

The Property Forum

COM   www.psa.co.ukforum/index.asp

This site has useful information and links on property related matters, in particular regarding conveyancing matters.

Ombudsman for Estate Agents

OFF   www.oea.co.uk

The Ombudsman can only investigate complaints against member estate agents. However, if you have a complaint against your estate agent relating to the buying and selling of residential property, you should consider using the Ombudsman.

Beckett House
4 Bridge Street
Salisbury
Wiltshire SP1 2LX
Tel: 01722 333 306
Fax: 01722 332 296
Email: post@oea.co.uk

Residential tenancies

Short leases

Although a substantial proportion of people now own their own homes, many people rent property, either from the local authority or one of the social housing authorities, or from a private landlord on a shorthold tenancy agreement. This area of law is very complex and tenants' rights will often depend on whether they have a private or a 'social' landlord and the date their tenancy started. However, all tenants have the right to live in the property undisturbed by their landlord, the right not to be evicted other than by a court order, and basic rights regarding the standard of repair of their property. Although you can consult a solicitor regarding all these problems, you can also consult the Tenancy Relations Officer at your local authority. They can write on your behalf to your landlord and may, in serious cases, arrange for a prosecution for unlawful eviction or for a repairs order to be served. Tenants can often get Legal Aid for housing problems, particularly if these involve unlawful eviction. Make sure you instruct a firm of solicitors which is experienced in housing law - it is best to choose a firm that has a Community Legal Service Quality Mark in housing law - use the Just Ask website or LSC call centre. Shelter can also give helpful advice - their details are under 'Homelessness' later in this section.

From the landlords' point of view, they sometimes feel that their rights are overridden by those of their tenants. However, they do normally have the right to evict troublesome tenants, or, if the tenancy agreement is a shorthold one, any tenant. But, they do have to comply properly with all the formalities and should therefore seek legal advice if they are unsure of the procedure. There is a number of legal requirements that landlords have to comply with generally, and new landlords should familiarise themselves with these before letting. If you need to consult a solicitor, choose a firm that is known to specialise in this area of work.

There is a **Legal Services Commission booklet** on renting and letting property. For information on how to obtain these leaflets, see the section on the Legal Services Commission in Part 2.

The Independent Housing Ombudsman

OFF www.ihos.org.uk

The IHO operates a complaints scheme for tenants of member landlords. Members include social landlords (but not Councils) and landlords who have registered voluntarily. There is a register online of member landlords. The IHO is currently also involved in a pilot Tenancy Deposit Scheme in certain parts of the country.

Norman House
105-109 Strand
London WC2R 0AA
Tel: 020 7836 3630
Lo call: 0845 7125 973
Fax: 020 7836 3900
Email: ombudsman@ihos.org.uk

Association of Residential Letting Agents (ARLA)

OFF www.arla.co.uk

This is a professional self-regulating body for letting agents. If a letting agent is a member of ARLA, certain standards must be adhered to and the company must have professional indemnity insurance. ARLA also operates a 'fidelity bond' service that enables landlords and tenants to recover money held by an agent. The website has useful information for both landlords and tenants, and you can search online for letting agents that are members.

Maple House
53-55 Woodside Road
Amersham
Bucks HP6 6AA
Tel: 01494 431 680
Fax: 01494 431 530
Email: info@arla.co.uk

The Rent Service

This deals, among other things, with the assessment of rents for protected tenancies and for Housing Benefit. To find your local Rent Officer ring 020 7388 4383.

Landlord-Law Online

COM www.landlordlaw.co.uk

This is a solicitors' website that specialises in private residential law for both landlords and tenants. There is a lot of information on the site and you can also instruct a solicitor at fixed rates. See also *Residential Lettings* guide, published by Law Pack.

Long leases

Many properties are held on long leases, in particular, flats. Tenants often encounter problems, for example, when their landlords impose unreasonable service charges. Generally, this type of problem is best dealt with by the tenants acting together, usually via residents' associations.

The Leasehold Advisory Service

OFF   www.lease-advice.org

If you have a problem regarding your lease, this should perhaps be your first port of call. It is an independent advice agency that provides free advice. The website has information about the service and a number of extremely helpful articles and reports. Follow the link 'find out more about LEASE'.

70-74 City Road
London EC1Y 2BJ
Tel: 020 7490 9580
Fax: 020 7253 2043
Email: info@lease-advice.org

The telephone lines are open between 10am and 1pm and between 2pm and 5pm, Monday to Friday. Letters and emails can usually be replied to within ten working days.

Homelessness

If you are threatened with eviction, whether by your landlord or by your mortgage lender, it is most important that you do not move out of your home until you have taken legal advice. You may be eligible to be re-housed by the local authority, but will lose that right if they consider that you are 'voluntarily homeless' because you have moved out before you had to. Contact the Homelessness Officer at your local authority. The local authority will normally have a duty to re-house you if you are pregnant, have dependent children living with you, or are vulnerable as a result of old age, mental illness or handicap, physical disability or some other special reason. If they refuse to re-house you, seek legal advice, as sometimes the courts can overturn their decision. If you are on a low income or on benefit you will be entitled to free legal advice. Make sure you chose a firm of solicitors that specialises in housing work.

Note that some courts now have an arrangement with local advice agencies who run a free advice service at court for people who are being evicted. You are best advised, however, to seek advice well before this stage.

There is a **Legal Services Commission booklet** on losing your home. For information on how to obtain these leaflets, see the section on the Legal Services Commission in Part 2.

Shelter

NFP www.shelter.org.uk

The main charity on all housing matters. Their website contains much useful information and links to other organisations.

For housing help and advice contact the 24 hour helpline Shelterline, 0808 800 4444. The helpdesk is open between 9am and 5.30pm, Monday to Friday and between 9am and 1pm, Saturday.
Email: info@shelter.org.uk

Shelter also has a network of local Housing Aid Centres around England which you can visit to get advice and information. To find the one nearest to you call 020 7505 2000.

Shelter Cymru provides information and advice for people in Wales. Tel: 01792 469 400.

Business tenancies

Although the underlying principles are the same, business tenancies operate under different legislation to residential tenancies and different rules apply. It is important that you get legal advice when taking on any sort of business tenancy, even if it is only short term. For example, the agreement you sign may contain onerous repairing obligations. You should also note that if you fail to pay your rent your landlord still has the right to forfeit your lease and take possession, without getting a court order (unlike residential tenancies). The best place to get advice on business tenancies is from a solicitor.

Planning

Most people's involvement with the planning legislation is in connection with alterations and extensions with their houses. Your builder or architect, who will also deal with the relevant building regulations, will usually deal with obtaining planning permission. It is important to understand that building regulations and planning regulations are different and compliance with one does not necessarily mean compliance with the other. If you do need to consult a solicitor about planning law, you should try to choose a solicitor who is on the Planning Panel.

The Planning Portal Programme

GOV www.planningportalprogramme.gov.uk

This is part of the Government online service and has information and links relating to planning matters.

Planning Applications

COM www.planning-applications.co.uk

A very useful site, by surveyor Ian Butter, which guides you through the process of making a planning application.

Planning Advice

COM www.planningadvice.co.uk

This is a very useful website with lots of information on planning matters, set up by solicitors Denton Wilde Sapte.

Boundary & neighbour disputes

These can be very upsetting and are often extremely difficult to resolve. Perhaps one of the main reasons for this is that they often involve a personality clash with both sides taking entrenched positions. Lawyers and judges often dislike boundary disputes, the main reasons being the strong personal element, the fact that the clients frequently do not really understand the very complex legal points that are often involved, the fact that these complex legal points are usually not the real problem (which is generally that the personalities of the neighbours are incompatible), the fact that most disputes are often over small areas of land or matters which seem petty to outsiders, and the fact that the legal costs generally end up being grossly disproportionate to the value of the land involved. If you have a neighbour problem, you should try to avoid going to law. The best method of resolving neighbour disputes, and the one that is most likely to actually address the underlying issues, is mediation. See the Mediation section for further information on this.

The Boundary Problems Website

COM   www.boundaries-maynard.cwc.net/index.htm

This helpful site set up by surveyor Jon Maynard has much useful information on boundary disputes and how to avoid or deal with them.

Garden Law

COM   www.gardenlaw.co.uk

A very useful site where you can find out what you can and cannot do in your garden.

General property websites

The Land Registry

GOV   www.landregistrydirect.gov.uk

Most land in England and Wales is now registered at the Land registry and these records can be accessed by the pubic, normally for a fee. You can get the information either from the Land Registry Direct website or by telephone or post.

There is a number of land registries covering different areas in England and Wales, and when applying for information by post or telephone, you will need to make your application to the correct land registry for the property you are enquiring about.

Tel: 020 7917 5939
Email: admin@landregistrydirect.gov.uk

The Lands Tribunal

GOV   www.courtservice.gov.uk/tribunals/lands_frm.htm

The Lands Tribunal is a court of law established to determine questions of disputed compensation arising out of the compulsory acquisition of land, to decide rating appeals, to exercise jurisdiction under Section 84 of the Law of Property Act 1925 (discharge and modification of restrictive covenants), and to act as arbitrator under references by consent. This site contains information about The Lands Tribunal and how to bring a case, details of the relevant regulations, and some case law.

Scottish law

Scotland has a different legal system from England and Wales, although the ultimate court of appeal for both is the House of Lords. If you have a problem that involves Scottish law, you will need to use a Scottish lawyer. A good way to find one is through the Law Society of Scotland. Details are also given below of a leading Scottish legal charity, the Legal Services Agency Ltd Scotland. You should be able to get helpful information on your problem from one or other of these organisations, particularly if you are able to access their websites. See also Delia Venables's site which has a special section on Scottish legal resources.

The Law Society of Scotland

OFF   www.lawscot.org.uk

This is the counterpart of the Law Society of England and Wales. Their very helpful website has information about the Scottish legal system and law, and a complete listing of all firms of solicitors in Scotland. The Society also deals with complaints against Scottish solicitors in their Client Relations Office.

Dial-a-law - 0870 545 5554 is a service offered by the Society which will help you find a Scottish solicitor.

26 Drumsheugh Gardens
Edinburgh EH3 7YR
Tel: 0131 226 7411
Fax: (Gp 2 & 3) 0131 225 2934
Email: lawscot@lawscot.org.uk

Client Relations Office Helpline
Tel: 0131 476 8137
Fax: 0131 225 2934
Email: cro@nildram.co.uk

The Scottish Legal Aid Board

OFF www.slab.org.uk

There is a legal aid system in Scotland similar to that in England and Wales. Further information can be obtained from the website or by contacting the Scottish Legal Aid Board direct.

44 Drumsheugh Gardens
Edinburgh EH3 7SW
Tel: 0131 226 7061

The Legal Services Agency Ltd Scotland

NFP www.lsa.org.uk

This is Scotland's leading law centre and is a charity seeking to assist those in disadvantage, particularly in the areas of housing and social welfare law. Initial advice on all legal matters is free. There is a drop-in service at the Glasgow office most Wednesdays between 1.30pm and 3.30pm. The website is excellent and you can download informative leaflets on various topics. There is also a criminal injuries calculator on the site.

134 Renfrew Street
Glasgow
Scotland G3 6ST
Tel: 0141 353 3354 - ring this number for an appointment with a lawyer. You can also ring for general advice most Wednesday or Thursday mornings, 11am to 1pm.

Senior citizens

There are particular types of problems associated with older people, for example, pension problems, entitlement to medical services and the like. If you have any type of property (for example, if you own a house or flat), you should make a will. Do take some advice before doing this - it is easy to make a mistake (and of course this will probably only come to light when it is too late to do anything about it). The last thing your loved ones need when dealing with the grief of your death are legal problems regarding your will. The two organisations below will be able to assist, both with making a will and other problems. In particular, if you are a 'grey surfer' you should certainly visit the Help the Aged site, which is very comprehensive. See also the section on Wills, Trusts, and Probate below.

Help the Aged

NFP www.helptheaged.org.uk

REC A very well-known organisation that gives advice and practical support to elderly people. The website contains a vast amount of information on practical matters for older people, such as financial information and writing a will. There is also a shopping section.

Head Office:
207-221 Pentonville Road
London N1 9UZ
Tel advice line: 0808 800 6565 (freephone). Lines are open between 9am and 4pm, Monday to Friday.
Tel: 020 7278 1114
Fax: 020 7278 1116
Email: info@helptheaged.org.uk

Solicitors for the Elderly

NFP www.solicitorsfortheelderly.com

COM This is the website of a national not-for-profit association of lawyers who are concerned with the availability of delivery of legal services to older people. You can use their database to find a specialist solicitor near to you. The site also has a very good links page.

Contact:
Bearders Solicitors
5 King Street
Brighouse
West Yorkshire HD6 1NX
Tel/Fax: 01422 822 737
Email: info@solicitorsfortheelderly.com

Pensions Ombudsman

GOV www.pensions-ombudsman.org.uk

Considers complaints of misadministration by, and disputes of fact or law with, trustees, managers, employers and administrators in relation to pension schemes. Schemes can be 'occupational' (i.e. established by an employer) or 'personal' (set up by an individual for themselves), and his jurisdiction includes 'stakeholder' pensions. In some circumstances, he can investigate complaints made by trustees, managers or employers against similar bodies. The present Pensions Ombudsman is Dr Julian Farrand. There is no charge for using the Ombudsman's services. Further information can be obtained from the website.

11 Belgrave Road
London SW1V 1RB
Tel: 020 7834 9144
Fax: 020 7821 0065
Email: enquiries@pensions-ombudsman.org.uk

Tax & VAT

Strictly speaking, problems with tax and VAT are not generally 'legal problems' although of course you will suffer the full force of the legal enforcement system if you fail to pay! For complex problems it is best to consult an accountant. However, the websites below will provide some help.

The Inland Revenue

GOV
REC

www.inlandrevenue.gov.uk

This is the Inland Revenue home site where you can find extensive information about tax and national insurance in the United Kingdom. You can also download forms and explanatory leaflets. A very useful site if you are completing your own tax forms or if you require any information about tax matters.

Customs and Excise/VAT

GOV
REC

www.hmce.gov.uk

This is the Customs and Excise home site and here you should be able to find all the information you need on VAT matters. There are contact details and helplines for various types of enquiry or problem. They also operate a general national telephone advice service.

National Advice Service: 0845 010 9000 open between 8am and 8pm, Monday to Friday.

Customs Confidential: 0800 59 5000 - to report smuggling, suspected fraud, or other suspicious activity; call in confidence, 24 hours a day, seven days a week.

The Adjudicator's Office

OFF www.adjudicatorsoffice.gov.uk

The Adjudicator's Office was set up in 1993 to investigate complaints about the way that the Inland Revenue and the Valuation Office Agency handle taxpayers' affairs. Since then, the office has taken on responsibility for looking into complaints about the Contributions Agency, now the National Insurance Contributions Office of the Inland Revenue, and Customs and Excise on VAT matters. The website has a FAQ page.

Haymarket House
28 Haymarket
London SW1Y 4SP
Tel: 020 7930 2292
Fax: 020 7930 2298
Email: adjudicators@gtnet.gov.uk

Welfare benefits

The benefits system in this country is very complex, which means that many people find it difficult to claim all that they are entitled to. If you are worried about this, perhaps the best place to go for advice is your local CAB or debt advice service, who are usually very knowledgeable. Generally, solicitors are less helpful here as this is not an area they traditionally work in. The organisations listed below will be able to give assistance.

There is a **Legal Services Commission booklet** on welfare benefits. For information on how to obtain these leaflets, see the section on the Legal Services Commission in Part 2.

Department of Social Security

GOV www.dss.gov.uk/index.htm

This website has extensive information about benefits.

War Pensions Agency

GOV www.dss.gov.uk/wpa

The War Pensioners' Welfare Service (WPWS) exists to provide advice, guidance and practical help to war disablement pensioners and war widows. They will try to help with any kind of welfare problem. It does not have to be directly linked to war disablement or service in HM Forces. The website has information about war pensions and how to claim.

War Pensions Agency
Norcross
Blackpool FY5 3WP
Tel: 0800 169 2277
Email: warpensions@gtnet.gov.uk

Wills, trusts & probate

Everyone should make a will, particularly if they have children or own property. Many people refuse to make a will or put it off, feeling that it somehow brings them closer to death. However, death will come to us all sooner or later. It is much better for those left behind that there is a clear will setting out the deceased's wishes, not only on how their property should be divided, but also on how their body should be dealt with (cremated, buried, the type of funeral service, whether their body parts can be used for medical purposes, etc.), and who should be appointed guardian for their children. Many people also like to make bequests to charities in their will.

The property and other assets you die possessed of are known as your 'estate'. The person who makes the will is known as the 'testator', and the people who benefit under the will are known as 'beneficiaries'. The people who administer your estate after you die are known as your 'personal representatives'. If they are appointed by a will they are known as 'executors'; if there is no will they are known as 'administrators'. A person dying leaving no will is said to have died 'intestate'.

If you do not make a will, your property will be dealt with under the general law. Basically, this provides for a large proportion of your estate (and for smaller estates, all of it) to go to your spouse with the balance (if any) in equal parts to your children. If you have no children, a larger proportion will go to your spouse (if you have one) and the balance (if any) to other relatives. If you have only a spouse but no children or relatives, then everything will go to your spouse. If you have no spouse or relatives, your estate will go to the Crown.

There are many organisations which will write a will for you, usually for a modest cost, or you can buy will forms in most stationers, or use Law Pack's *Last Will and Testament* book. However, in the opinion of the writer, unless your will is a very simple one, it is really best to get it drafted by a solicitor. Most solicitors will draft a simple will for quite a low fee, and during 'Make a Will Week' some solicitors firms offer to draft wills for free. If you are well off, you should also have professional advice, before you make your will, on how your estate can be dealt with in the most tax effective way after your death. Again, this is something that your solicitor can advise you on.

You should always review the provisions of your will at least every five years, or whenever your circumstances change, and consider whether you need to make a new will. Note that if you get married, you will always need to make a new will, as your existing one will become invalid.

When making a will, you will need to appoint at least one person (and preferably at least two, just in case one of them dies before you) to act as your executor. The executors will deal with sorting out your affairs, paying your debts, and distributing any remaining assets to your beneficiaries after you are dead. If your estate is reasonably large (for example, if you own your own home), and particularly if you have children, it is often a good idea to have a 'professional executor'. This is usually a solicitor, but can also be someone from a bank or building society or similar organisation. When a professional executor is appointed, you should be aware that they will make a charge for their services, and charges can be quite high. Again, in the opinion of the writer, it is usually best to appoint a solicitor executor, as they will always have indemnity insurance, and their charges, if excessive, can be challenged by requesting a 'remuneration certificate' from the Law Society (see the section on Solicitors in Part 2 above).

Testators will sometimes leave property 'in trust' for someone, most commonly when property is left to children under 18. The 'trustees' will legally own the property which is held 'in trust' for the 'beneficiary'. The trustees will manage the property for them for the duration of the trust - for children this will be until at least until their 18th birthday. Generally, the income from any property will be used for the beneficiaries' maintenance and the trustees will normally have powers to advance all or part of the capital for the beneficiaries if they think it appropriate. It is of course extremely important that the trustees are people you can rely on as, if you die when the children are young, they will be an important part of their life. Again, you should consider having a 'professional trustee' such as a solicitor who you can be sure will administer the trust responsibly and for the benefit of the child/children, but again you must take into account the fact that they will charge for their services. Your solicitor should explain all this in more detail at the time you make your will.

If you find that someone has appointed you executor, you will have to deal with obtaining the grant of probate and administering the estate. If you are not sure what to do, you can always get some general advice from a solicitor, even if you want to administer the estate yourself. Sometimes people will instruct a solicitor just to get the grant of probate (or 'letters of administration' where the deceased dies intestate), and deal with the rest of the work themselves. However, with a more complex estate, it is always worth considering getting a solicitor to act for you. Administering an estate can be a time consuming and also stressful business, particularly if you are unfamiliar with the procedures and are still grieving for the loss of a loved one. Make sure, however, that you use a solicitor who is familiar with this type of work and make sure that you are given full information about the solicitors' charges before you let him do any work.

Some solicitors will accept instructions online for drafting wills and obtaining grants of probate. Most of these can be found via Delia Venables's website.

There is a **Legal Services Commission booklet** on wills and probate. For information on how to obtain these leaflets, see the section on the Legal Services Commission in Part 2.

Probate Registries

This is where you obtain the grant of probate or letters of administration. There are probate registries in most cities and larger towns. To find the one nearest to you:

Tel: 0870 241 0109

Probates Direct

COM
REC www.probatesdirect.co.uk

This is a service set up by the Lister Croft Partnership, solicitors in Wakefield, Yorkshire. There is an 'advice centre' which gives helpful information on bereavement, useful contact details and information on some helpful books. You can use their service to obtain a grant of probate online, at a modest fee. This is a very good website for people seeking more information about what should be done when someone dies.

James Kessler

COM www.kessler.co.uk

For those of you willing to tackle more esoteric information, James Kessler, a barrister, has a website giving information about drafting trusts and will trusts. There is also a useful section on charities.

The Funeral Ombudsman

OFF www.funeralombudsman.org.uk

This Ombudsman investigates complaints against funeral directors and private crematoria that are members of the scheme, and awards compensation where appropriate. The scheme covers a substantial proportion of the UK funeral profession. If you have a complaint, the website has useful information and there is an online form you can print off and use.

26-28 Bedford Row
London WC1R 4HE
Tel: 020 7430 1112
Fax: 020 7430 1012
Email: fos@dircon.co.uk

Conclusion

This is the first edition of the Law Pack *Legal Advice Handbook*. I hope that you have found it useful.

During the period up to August 2002, I will be monitoring new websites and advice agencies in preparation for the next edition of this book. If you have any comments on the book, for example if you found that some of the contacts or websites gave a poor service, or if you wish to recommend another organisation or website which you think should be included, feel free to email me at tessa@tjshepperson.co.uk; alternatively, if you thought that some of the narrative was unhelpful or if there are other areas of law you thought should be covered, or if you are from one of the organisations mentioned and wish to correct your entry, your comments would be welcome. All emails will be considered and taken into account in preparation for the next edition.

I should also be interested in feedback on the articles, whether you found them helpful or not, and in suggestions for topics for the next edition.

Tessa Shepperson

List of Law Centres

Avon and Bristol Law Centre
2 Moon Street
Bristol BS2 8QE
0117 924 8662 (T)
0117 924 8020 (F)
Email: mail@ablc.demon.co.uk

Barnet Law Service (Law Centre)
9 Bell Lane
London NW4 2BP
020 8203 4141 (T)
020 8203 8042 (F)

Battersea Law Centre
(Attached to Wandsworth & Merton Law Centre)
14 York Road
London SW11 3QA
020 7228 9462 (T)
020 7978 5348 (F)
Email: GIH70@dial.pipex.com

Belfast Law Centre
See: Law Centre (Northern Ireland)

Bradford Law Centre
31 Manor Row
Bradford BD1 4PX
01274 306 617 (T)
01274 390 939 (F)
Email: enquiries@bradfordlawcentre.co.uk

Brent Community Law Centre
389 High Road Willesden
London NW10 2JR
020 8451 1122 (T)
020 8830 2462 (F)
Email: brentlaw@brentlaw.demon.co.uk

Camden Community Law Centre
2 Prince of Wales Road
London NW5 3LG
020 7485 6672 (T)
020 7267 6218 (F)
Email: admin@cclc.org.uk

Cardiff Law Centre
41/42 Clifton Street
Cardiff CF24 1LS
029 20498 117 (T)
029 20497 118 (F)
Email: cardiff.lawcentre@dial.pipex.com

Carlisle Law Centre
8 Spencer Street
Carlisle CA1 1BG
01228 515 129 (T)
01228 515 819 (F)
Email: information@communitylaw.org.uk

Central London Law Centre
19 Whitcomb Street
London WC2H 7HA
020 7839 2998 (T)
020 7839 6158 (F)

Chesterfield Law Centre
44 Park Road
Chesterfield S40 1XZ
01246 550 674 (T)
01246 551 069 (F)
Email:chesterfieldlawcentre@dial.pipex.com

Coventry Law Centre
The Bridge
Broadgate
Coventry CV1 1NG
024 7622 3053 (T)
024 7622 8551 (F)
Email: enquiries@covlaw.org.uk

Derby Law Centre
P.O Box 173
The Market Hall
Derby DE1 9XN
01332 344 557 (T)
01332 370 606 (F)
Email:derbylaw@dial.pipex.com

Devon Law Centre
Virginia House
40 Looe Street
Plymouth
Devon PL4 0EB
01752 519 794 (T)
01752 267 939 (F)
Email:information@devonlawcentre.org,uk

Gateshead Law Centre
1 Walker Terrace
Gateshead NE8 1EB
0191 477 1109 (T)
0191 477 7667 (F)
Email: glc@connectingbusiness.com

Gloucester Law Centre
75-81 Eastgate Street
Gloucester GL1 1PN
01452 423 492 (T)
01452 387 594 (F)
Email: gloslawcentre@dial.pipex.com

Greenwich Community Law Centre
187 Trafalgar Road
London SE10 9EQ
020 8853 2550 (T)
020 8853 5253 (F)
Email: greenwichcommunitylawcentre@
greenwichcommunity.freeserve.co.uk

Hackney Community Law Centre
8 Lower Clapton Road
London E5 0PD
020 8985 8364 (T)
020 8533 2018 (F)

Hammersmith & Fulham Law Centre
142/144 King Street
London W6 0QU
020 8741 4021 (T)
020 8741 1450 (F)
Email: hflaw@hflaw.org.uk

Harehills & Chapeltown
Law Centre
263 Roundhay Road
Leeds LS8 4HS
0113 249 1100 (T)
0113 235 1185 (F)
Email: admin@leedslawcentre.co.uk

Hillingdon Law Centre
12 Harold Avenue, Hayes
Middlesex UB3 4QW
020 8561 9400 (T)
020 8756 0837 (F)
Email: hillingdon@lawyersonline.co.uk

Hounslow Law Centre
51 Lampton Road
Hounslow
Middlesex TW3 1JG
020 8570 9505 (T)
020 8572 0730 (F)
Email: hounslowlc@dial.pipex.com

Humberside Law Centre
95 Alfred Gelder Street
Hull HU1 1EP
01482 211 180 (T)
01482 589 036 (F)
Email: hlc@hlc.demon.co.uk

Islington Law Centre
161 Hornsey Road
London N7 6DU
020 7607 2461 (T)
020 7700 0072 (F)
Email: info@is-law.org.uk

Law Centre (Northern Ireland)
124 Donegall Street
Belfast BT1 2GY
028 9024 4401 (T)
028 90223 6340 (F)
Email: lawcentre.belfast@cinni.org

Law Centre (Northern Ireland) Western Area
9 Clarendon Street
Londonderry BT48 7EP
028 7126 2433 (T)
028 7126 2343 (F)
Email: admin.derry@cinni.org

Leicester Law Centre
1st Floor
International House
Leicester LE1 6FD
0116 255 3781 (T)
0116 255 6431 (F)
Email: leicesterlawcentre@dial.pipex.com

Lewisham Law Centre
28 Deptford High Street
London SE8 3NU
020 8692 5355 (T)
020 8694 2516 (F)
Email: lewisham.law.centre@dial.pipex.com

Liverpool 8 Law Centre
34/36 Princes Road
Liverpool L8 1TH
0151 709 7222 (T)
0151 708 8178 (F)
Email: L8lawcentre@netscapeonline.co.uk

Luton Law Centre
28 Clarendon Road
Luton LU2 7PQ
01582 481 000 (T)
01582 482 581 (F)
Email: lutonlawcentre@ukonline.co.uk

Newcastle Law Centre
51 Westgate Road
Newcastle Upon Tyne NE1 1SG
0191 230 4777 (T)
0191 233 0295 (F)
Email: newcastle.law.centre@dial.pipex.com

Newham Rights Law Centre
285 Romford Road
London E7 9HJ
020 8555 3331 (T)
020 8519 7348 (F)
Email: newrlc.newhamrightslawcentre.
freeserve.co.uk

North Kensington Law Centre
74 Golborne Road
London W10 5PS
020 8969 7473 (T)
020 8968 0934 (F)

North Lambeth Law Centre
14 Bowden Street
London SE11 5DS
020 7582 4373 (T)
020 7582 2148 (F)
Email: nllc@excite.co.uk
London Race Discrimination Unit
Advice Line: 020 7582 4425

North Manchester Law Centre
Harpurhey District Centre
Off Rochdale Road
Harpurhey
Manchester M9 4DH
0161 205 9031 (T)
0161 205 8654 (F)
Email: nmlc@dial.pipex.com

Nottingham Law Centre
119 Radford Road
Nottingham NG7 5DU
0115 978 7813 (T)
0115 979 2969 (F)
Email: nottlawcent@dial.pipex.com

Oldham Law Centre
First Floor
Archway House
Bridge Street
Oldham Ol1 1ED
0161 627 0925 (T)
0161 620 3411 (F)
Email: lc-oldham@mcr1.poptel.org.uk

Paddington Law Centre
439 Harrow Road
London W10 4RE
020 8960 3155 (T)
020 8968 0417 (F)
Email: paddingtonlaw@dial.pipex.com

Plumstead Community
Law Centre
105 Plumstead High Street
London SE18 1SB
020 8855 9817 (T)
020 8316 7903 (F)
Email: PCLC@dial.pipex.com

Rochdale Law Centre
Smith Street
Rochdale OL16 1HE
01706 657 766 (T)
01706 346 558 (F)
Email: gll21@dial.pipex.com

Saltley & Nechells Law Centre
2 Alum Rock Road
Saltley
Birmingham B8 1JB
0121 328 2307 (T)
0121 327 7486 (F)
Email: saltleynechells.lawcentre@virgin.net

Sheffield Law Centre
First Floor
Waverley House
10 Joiner Street
Sheffield S3 8GW
0114 273 1888 (T)
0114 273 1501 (F)
Email: sheffieldlawcentre@dial.pipex.com

South Manchester Law Centre
584 Stockport Road
Manchester M13 0RQ
0161 225 5111 (T)
0161 225 0210 (F)
Email: admin@smlc.org.uk

Southwark Law Centre
Hanover Park House
14-16 Hanover Park
Peckham
London SE15 5HS
020 7732 2008 (T)
020 7732 2034 (F)
Email: southwark.law.centre@dial.pipex.com

Springfield Law Centre
Springfield Hospital
Glenburnie Road
London SW17 7DJ
020 8767 6884 (T)
020 8767 6996 (F)
Email: thelawcentre@springfieldhospital.
freeserve.co.uk

Thamesmead Law Centre
(Attached to Plumstead Community Law
Centre)
St Paul's Churchyard
Bentham Road
London SE28
020 8311 0555 (T)
020 8311 0515 (F)

Tottenham Law Centre
63 Grand Parade
Green Lanes
London N4 1AF
020 8800 1315 (T)
020 8800 5443 (F)

Tower Hamlets Law Centre
214 Whitechapel Road
London E1 1BG
020 7247 8998 (T)
020 7247 9424 (F)
Email: gic21@dial.pipex.com

Vauxhall Law and Information Centre
C/o The VNC Millennium Resource Centre
Blenheim Street
Liverpool L5 8UX
0151 330 0239 (T)
0151 207 4948 (F)

Wandsworth & Merton Law Centre
101a Tooting High Street
London SW17 0SU
020 8767 2777 (T)
020 8767 2711 (F)
Email: lawcentre@wamlawcentre.fsnet.co.uk

Warrington Law Centre
64/66 Bewsey Street
Warrington
Cheshire WA2 7JQ
01925 651 104 (T)
01925 444 736 (F)
Email: warrington@dial.pipex.com

Wiltshire Law Centre
Temple House
115-118 Commercial Road
Swindon SN1 5PL
01793 486 926 (Voice and Minicom)
01793 432 193 (F)
Email: wiltslawcentre@dial.pipex.com

Wythenshawe Law Centre
260 Brownley Road
Wythenshawe
Manchester M22 5EB
0161 498 0905/6 (T)
0161 498 0750   (F)
Email: info@wlawcentre.co.uk

AIRE
Advice on Individual Rights in Europe
74 Euro Link
Business Centre
49 Effra Road
London SW2 1BZ
020 7924 0927 (T)
020 7733 6786 (F)
Email: aire@btinternet.com

Cambridge House Legal Centre
137 Camberwell Road
London SE5 0HF
020 7701 9499 (T)
020 7703 3051 (F)

Castlemilk Law and Money Advice Centre
30-32 Dougrie Drive
Castlemilk
Glasgow G45 9AD
0141 634 0313 (T)
0141 634 1944 (F)
Email: castlemilk@lawcentre1.freeserve.co.uk

LCF Associate Members

Disability Law Service
Ground Floor
39-45 Cavell Street
London E1 2BP
020 7791 9800 (T)
020 7791 9802 (F)
020 7791 9801 (Minicom)
Email: advice@dls.org.uk

EarthRights
Little Orchard
School Lane
Mole Hill Green
Takeley
Essex CM22 69J
07071 225011 (T)
Email: earthrights@gn.apc.org

Free Legal Advice Centre (Ireland)
49 South William Street
Dublin 2
Eire
353 1679 4239 (T)
353 1679 1554 (F)

Greater Manchester Immigration Aid Unit
400 Cheetham Hill Road
Manchester M8 9LE
0161 740 7722 (T)
0161 740 5172 (F)

Mary Ward Legal Centre
26-27 Boswell Street
London WC1N 3JZ
020 7831 7079 (T)
020 7831 5431 (F)
Email: info@marywardcentre.ac.uk
Website: www.marywardcentre.ac.uk

For Law Centres based in Scotland, please contact:

Scottish Association of Law Centres
C/o Drumchapel Law & Money Advice Centre
Unit 28, 42 Dalsetter Avenue
Drumchapel, Glasgow G15 8TE
0141 944 0507 (T)
0141 944 7605 (F)
Email: law@dlmc.freeserve.co.uk

Index